PETER W. NESSELROTH

LAUTREAMONT'S IMAGERY

A STYLISTIC APPROACH

LIBRAIRIE DROZ, GENÈVE - PARIS

1969

HISTOIRE DES IDÉES
ET CRITIQUE LITTÉRAIRE

VOL. 96

PETER W. NESSELROTH

LAUTRÉAMONT'S IMAGERY

A *STYLISTIC APPROACH*

GENÈVE
LIBRAIRIE DROZ
11, RUE MASSOT
—
1969

© 1969 by Librairie Droz
11, rue Massot, Genève (Switzerland)

To the memory of my father.

FOREWORD

This study attempts to analyze an aspect of Lautréamont's style which, until now, has only been treated in an impressionistic manner.

Among my teachers at Columbia University, I wish to thank, in particular, Professor Michael Riffaterre for his guidance, encouragement and forbearance, and Professor Jean Hytier for his kindness and understanding. I am also grateful to Professor Gaston Gille, of The City College of New York, whose continued interest in the progress of my work provided the necessary incentive.

Finally, I would like to express my gratitude to all my friends and colleagues, in the Department of Romance Languages of The City College, for their helpful comments and suggestions.

———

TABLE OF CONTENTS

INTRODUCTION

Lautréamont's influence on surrealist imagery is a commonplace in anthologies of contemporary poetry. C. A. Hackett, for instance, writes that "Lautréamont provided the surrealists with a mass of material drawn from the unconscious mind; a fresh technique—the *écriture automatique*; and a new idea of beauty based on unusual associations, such as the celebrated 'beau comme ... la rencontre fortuite sur une table de dissection d'une machine à coudre et d'un parapluie.' " [1] Unfortunately, even histories of surrealism usually restrict themselves to a short, impressionistic comment: "Lautréamont's imagery, its hallucinatory force, the subconscious trains of thought which it reveals, its occasional basis in the absurd create a point of contact with the surrealists." [2]

The need for a systematic study of Lautréamont's style in general and of his imagery in particular, has often been stated. Edmond Jaloux, in his introduction to the 1938 Corti edition, remarked: "Il y aurait une étude particulière à écrire aussi sur le style de Lautréamont. Il est à la fois classique et neuf, romantique et prophétique. Dans une forme rigoureusement et purement traditionnelle, il fait entrer les images les plus inattendues et les plus hardies, tout un luxe de rapprochements d'idées et de métaphores inattendues, qui plus tard donnera naissance à un véritable monde poétique." [3] And Suzanne Bernard: "Cette frénésie agissante, par laquelle Lautréamont se libère de toutes les contraintes, sociales ou religieuses, exerce sur le style aussi son action libératrice: de la manière la plus consciente, Lautréamont applique sa volonté anarchique aux rapports des mots entre eux, les soumet (aussi bien que les créatures de son univers poétique,

---

[1] *Anthology of Modern French Poetry* (New York, 1952), p. 214.
[2] Anna Balakian, *Surrealism: The Road to the Absolute* (New York, 1959), p. 22.
[3] Lautréamont, *Œuvres complètes* (José Corti, 1958), p. 35. All the quotations from Lautréamont are taken from this edition, which includes the prefaces to other editions by Léon Genonceaux, Remy de Gourmont, Edmond Jaloux, André Breton, Philippe Soupault, Julien Gracq, Roger Caillois and Maurice Blanchot.

en voie de perpétuelle métamorphose) à ce qu'André Breton appelle 'un principe de mutation perpétuelle': et je songe surtout, ici, à l'emploi qu'il fait de la métaphore, et dont une étude particulière est nécessaire pour pénétrer l'essence du génie poétique ducassien." [4]

Instead, most commentators have concerned themselves with problems of biography or of sources. [5] And the best studies which have dealt with the work itself, Léon Pierre-Quint's *Le Comte de Lautréamont et Dieu*, Bachelard's *Lautréamont* and Blanchot's *Lautréamont et Sade*, have provided perceptive insights more through the brilliant intuitions of their authors than through a close textual analysis. [6] Bachelard begins his book by referring to the animal content in *Les Chants de Maldoror*, but he uses it for his own type of thematic interpretation and does not provide a detailed study of the imagery itself. Yet, if only for the lack of any other meaningful evidence, Lautréamont can be approached in no other way but through his writing: "*Les Chants de Maldoror* ainsi se dérobent à toute entreprise qui ne les considère pas d'abord dans la matérialité première-dernière, seule preuve enfin de leur existence (pour nous), leur écriture," writes Marcelin Pleynet. "Nous devons d'abord, et avant toute autre chose, poser leur manifestation d'écriture, puisque c'est d'abord, et avant toute autre chose, et seulement, en tant qu'écriture qu'ils nous arrivent. Je veux dire, et la chose toute banale qu'elle paraisse est loin d'être facile à accepter, que dans la mesure où ils déçoivent toute interprétation, nous ne pouvons considérer *Les Chants de Maldoror* que parce qu'ils sont écrits. Nous n'avons rien à leur faire dire qu'ils ne disent pas et ils ne disent rien d'autre que leur écriture." [7] And the same author comments, further in the book, "et il faut (je souligne bien), il faut s'interroger sur l'absence, depuis bientôt un siècle, de question rhétorique chez les commentateurs de Lautréamont; alors que tous les problèmes soulevés par *Les Chants* trouvent là leur aboutissement." [8]

---

[4] *Le Poème en prose de Baudelaire jusqu'à nos jours* (Paris, 1959), p. 243.
[5] For Lautréamont's biography, see Maurice Saillet's introduction to the Livre de Poche edition (Paris, 1963), pp. 7-32. See also Marcelin Pleynet, *Lautréamont par lui-même* (Paris, 1967), which has an excellent synopsis of the biographical research and an outline of the various source theories, pp. 98-99.
[6] Léon Pierre-Quint, *Le Comte de Lautréamont et Dieu* (Marseille, 1929). Gaston Bachelard, *Lautréamont* (Corti, 1939 and 1963). My quotations from Bachelard refer to the 1963 edition. Maurice Blanchot, *Lautréamont et Sade* (Les Editions de Minuit, 1949 and 1963). My quotations from Blanchot also refer to the 1963 edition.
[7] Pleynet, *op. cit.*, p. 109.
[8] *Ibid.*, p. 134.

The aim of the present study is to analyze the most noticeable feature of Lautréamont's style: his imagery. As I hope to show, this feature is so remarkable because it disrupts, by bringing together in one syntactical structure concrete and abstract words and literal and figurative usages, the reader's expectation of clearly defined categories of the sensual and the mental as well as of reality and imagination. The term "imagery" immediately raises problems of definition. Stephen Ullmann remarks that: "There is in particular a certain danger of confusion between 'image' in the sense of 'mental representation' and 'image' in the sense of 'figure of speech expressing some similarity or analogy'." [9] The sense which concerns us here is that of image as a figure of speech, that is, in the traditional sense of simile and metaphor.

Another problem is that of classification. Christine Brooke-Rose writes, in her introduction, that most of the attempts at classification throughout the history of rhetoric, from Aristotle to Richards, are based on idea-content, and can be divided into four main groups:

1) *The species/genus classification* (Aristotle)
2) *The animate/inanimate classification* (Aristotle's successors)
3) *The classification by domain of thought* (implicit in Cicero and some Renaissance rhetoricians, taken up by 19th and 20th century critics for detailed linguistic and literary analysis)
4) *The analysis by dominant trait* (Modern German School).[11]

In modern times, the most common approach is by thought domain, as in Edmond Huguet's *Les Comparaisons et les métaphores de Victor Hugo* (although he also uses the analysis by dominant trait, i.e. the similarity between the literal meaning and the metaphoric meaning) and Caroline Spurgeon's *Shakespeare's Imagery and What It Tells Us*. The main weakness of the method is that it is descriptive rather than critical, that it shows the "what and why" instead of the "what and how". Miss Spurgeon's research, for instance, had to

---

[9] Stephen Ullmann, "The Nature of Imagery" in *Language and Style* (New York, 1964), p. 176. This article appeared first in French under the title "L'Image littéraire. Quelques questions de méthode" in *Langue et littérature. Actes du VIII⁰ Congrès de la Fédération Internationale des Langues et Littératures Modernes* (Paris, 1961), pp. 41-49. It is the best overall view of the problem. See also, in the same volume, Gerald Antoine, "Pour une méthode d'analyse stylistique des images," pp. 151-164.

[11] *A Grammar of Metaphor* (London, 1958), p. 3.

wait for the critical evaluation of Cleanth Brooks to bring out its literary significance. [12] Moreover, these studies usually concern themselves more with the biography and psychology of the author than with the effect of the imagery on the addressee of the work, the reader.

A linguistic approach, such as Christine Brooke-Rose's, can yield much more fruitful results from a critical point of view. Her method attempts to reveal how the structure of the metaphor, in several poets, produces certain effects. She classifies metaphors into five main categories: " 1) *Simple Replacement*: the proper term is replaced altogether by the metaphor, without being mentioned at all.... 2) *The Pointing Formulae*: the proper term A is mentioned, then replaced by the metaphor B with some demonstrative expression pointing back to the proper term (A... that B).... 3) *The Copula*: a direct statement that A is B.... 4) *The link with 'To Make'*: a direct statement involving a third party: C makes A into B.... 5) *The Genitive* (in the very wide sense of provenance from): ...B *is part of,* or *derives from,* or *belongs to* or *is attributed to* or *is found in* C, from which relationship we can guess A, the proper term (e.g., the *hostel* of my heart [the body])." [13] This terminology is useful because, being based on grammatical links which are particular to metaphors, it takes into account the relationship between the literal and figurative elements. This is something which traditional grammatical categories are unable to do. But her system, I think, is more suitable for a general theory of metaphors (in which one can draw from more than one source to illustrate a point) than for the study of a particular poet. It must also be kept in mind that the effect of a device very often depends on its context and that, therefore, similar structures do not necessarily have the same affectivity.

Rather than adopting an *a priori* classification for my analysis of Lautréamont's images, I have thought it best to group them by what might be called their "striking characteristics". Since an image consists of a semantic level which is superimposed on a syntactic structure, either or both of these levels can produce an effect. To organize an analysis by either thought domain or structure would be artificial and incomplete because it would require the exclusion of important features for the sake of a pure system of classification. I have therefore arranged my examples according to the element of the

---

[12] See "The Naked Babe and the Cloak of Manliness" in *The Well Wrought Urn* (New York, 1947), pp. 22-49.
[13] *Grammar*, pp. 24-25.

image that is likely to catch the reader's attention first (and may consequently be its most superficial aspect). This can be a specific form—the Homeric analogical epithet—or the particular recurring thought domain—the animal similes. But even these categories could not be rigidly maintained: to be thorough I had to indicate cases where certain themes seem to provoke certain forms. It must be remembered that a system of classification is merely a convenience and that the text should not be subordinate to the method.

Within each category, I classified the examples of the same device according to their degree of salience. My approach is based on the stylistic theories of Michael Riffaterre, whose major principles can be outlined as follows: [14]

1) In the act of communication, the message appears as a verbal code. When this code is in writing, the message acquires permanence.

2) The encoder will see to it that "inescapable elements are unpredictable." This creates a series of binary oppositions between the predictable and the unpredictable, between the pattern and the contrast.

The intentions of the encoder (author), even if it were valid to appeal to them for the purpose of literary criticism, [15] cannot be established with certainty.

3) In style analysis, it is therefore better to rely on the decoder's (reader's) perception of the stylistic device (the unpredictable element). "For he [the reader] is the consciously selected target of the author; the stylistic device is so contrived that the reader cannot overlook it or even read without being guided by it to the essentials." [16]

---

[14] These theories are developed in a series of articles : "Criteria for Style Analysis, "*Word*, XV (1959), 154-174. "Stylistic Context," *Word*, XVI (1960), 207-208. "Problèmes d'analyse du style littéraire," *Romance Philology*, XIV (1961), 216-227. "Vers la définition linguistique du style," *Word*, XVII (1961), 318-344. "Comment décrire le style de Chateaubriand?," *RR*, LIII (1962), 128-138. The method was applied most recently in "Describing Poetic Structures: Two Approaches to Baudelaire's *Les Chats*," *YFS*, 36-37 (1966), 200-242. For critiques of the method, see Jean Mourot, "Stylistique des intentions et stylistiques des effets," *CAIEF*, 16 (1964), 71-79, who falls back on the intentional fallacy, and David Lodge, *Language of Fiction* (London: New York, 1966), pp. 58-60, whose objection seems to be that objective stylistic analysis is impossible.
[15] For a criticism of this approach to literature, see W. K. Wimsatt, Jr., "The Intentional Fallacy" in *The Verbal Icon* (University of Kentucky Press, 1954), pp. 3-18.
[16] "Criteria," p. 162.

Since the reader's reaction is likely to involve a subjective value judgment, the style investigator must disregard the content of that judgment and consider it only as a response to a stimulus, as *a signal*.

4) It is also necessary for the style investigator to consider the permanence of the encoded message and the changing code of reference of the reader. This makes it possible to account for varying effects, to correct modern readers' reactions and, for the critic and the historian, to explain a literary work's survival (instead of relying on the evolution of aesthetic norms or on the work's content).

5) The presence of stimuli is revealed by the response of *informants*: critical commentators, editors who have annotated the text, translators, etc., even the style investigator himself. But it is necessary to disregard, at least initially, the informant's interpretation, which may or may not be correct. "Stripped of its formulation in terms of value, the secondary response becomes an objective criterion for the existence of its stylistic stimulus." [17]

6) The sum of these informants, with their converging responses, constitutes *a superreader*. The style analyst uses this totality to locate the stylistically active devices in a text. The multiplication of evidence makes it possible to avoid giving undue importance to extra-textual factors (reader's fatigue, personal bias, etc.).

7) It is only after the stylistic device has been located and analyzed that it becomes possible to proceed to the interpretive level, to metastylistics.

In short, the aim of stylistic analysis is to avoid premature and impressionistic value judgments, by concentrating on description of verifiable elements in the text and by making this description as objective as possible. This does not mean that evaluation should be avoided altogether; it simply means that it should have an objective foundation: "Il ne s'agit pas de dénier au critique le goût et le droit de se servir de sa culture; il ne s'agit pas non plus d'envahir, statistique au poing, le domaine de l'esthéticien. Il s'agit de donner à leurs enquêtes une base objective, et d'éviter que leurs jugements de valeur soient pris pour des critères d'existence." [18]

Crucial in this theory is the concept of predictability and unpredictability. The reader brings to the text certain expectations which

---

[17] *Ibid.*, p. 163.
[18] "Problèmes d'analyse du style littéraire," p. 227, n. 29.

are either fulfilled or denied. In the case of imagery, he will expect to find resemblance in similes and, in metaphors, features that are common to both the word used figuratively and the word used literally. The more difficult it is to find the resemblance or the common features, the more striking will be the image. The context which precedes the image may, of course, decrease the difficulty by preparing the reader to understand or, on the contrary, increase it by creating a misleading pattern.

In my analysis, I have kept the traditional division of images into similes and metaphors. The difference has not always been taken into account by rhetoricians, but it exists and is of importance because they do not work the same way. In metaphors, some words are used literally and others figuratively. The image is produced by the interaction of these two levels. In similes, there are two sets of literal meanings, and the effect is created by the juxtaposition of the two sets. Saying "he rushed on like a lion" limits the attributes of "the lion", which apply to "he", to the verbal action "rushed on". Whereas saying "a lion, he rushed on" produces an effect of almost complete identification.

For similes I have followed I. A. Richard's terminology: the first part of the comparison is the *tenor* and the second *the vehicle*. [19] Other theoreticians have objected to the ambiguous use of the terms, when applied to metaphors, and Richards himself has not been able to keep a clear distinction between them. But, since similes consist of a two-part structure, the danger of confusion is greatly reduced. In this study, then, *tenor* refers to what, in French, is called *le comparé* and *vehicle* to *le comparant*. For metaphors, Max Black has suggested the words *focus* and *frame*. The *focus* is the expression which is used figuratively in a literal context. Thus in the statement "the chairman ploughed through the meeting", "ploughed" is the focus and the rest of the sentence is the frame, and this double unit of focus and frame is *the metaphorical statement*. [20] Since these terms suggest the interwoven nature of metaphors, I have found them to be generally adequate tools for metaphor analysis. [21] Moreover, the differenciation in terminology for similes and metaphors makes it

[19] *The Philosophy of Rhetoric* (New York, 1936), pp. 96-97.
[20] *Models and Metaphors* (Ithaca, 1962), pp. 27-28.
[21] For a critical commentary on Black, see Monroe C. Beardsley, *Aesthetics: Problems in the Philosophy of Criticism* (New York, 1958), pp. 134-147, and note 10-6, pp. 159-162.

possible to avoid such awkward terms as "the vehicle of the vehicle" and "the tenor of the tenor" in cases where metaphors and similes are combined. It may also be necessary to refer to the capacity of one object to enter into a metaphorical relation with another object. For this purpose I have adopted the term *link* as suggested by Winifred Nowottny, when the plausibility of connection is explicit. [22] When it is implicit, I have kept Richards' *ground* which refers to the common characteristics of the tenor and the vehicle. [23]

Generally, I have proceeded in three steps. First, I indicated the context in which the examples are located. For the information of my reader, it was sometimes necessary to paraphrase the text (the alternative would have been to quote excessively long passages). This is in no way to be considered as an analysis. Secondly, following the examples, there is the analysis proper which consists of a description of relevant features. Here, my aim was to be as objective and complete as possible. [24] And thirdly, I tried to evaluate what effect the image is likely to produce.

In the conclusion, an attempt was made to show how a detailed analysis of Lautréamont's imagery can be reconciled with broader interpretations and, since the emphasis was on the psychology of the reader, what the cultural implications of the work are.

---

[22] *The Language Poets Use* (London, 1962), p. 54.
[23] Richards, *Philosophy*, p. 117.
[24] To lessen subjectivity, I have used the *Larousse du XIXe siècle*, which gives the usual figurative meaning of words. These, by virtue of their often being platitudes, will presumably have the same connotations for the greatest number of readers. For present-day readers, I have verified my own impressions in the *Larousse du XXe siècle* and in Robert's *Dictionnaire alphabétique et analogique de la langue française*.

CHAPTER I

FORMAL SIMILES

Since the images which disrupt the reader's habits most violently are likely to catch his attention first, I thought it best to treat them in descending order of originality.

If we take as a guide I. A. Richards' statement that the interest of a metaphor depends usually as much on the disparity between the two members related by a metaphor as on their likeness [1], then the most striking of Lautréamont's similes are the ones in the "beau comme" series. This is the type of image which fits André Breton's definition "l'image... la plus forte est celle qui présente le degré d'arbitraire le plus élevé..." [2] and which has had the greatest influence on the surrealist poets.

The comparison is characterized by a growing distance between the tenor ("beau comme" in apposition to a noun or as an attribute) and one or several vehicles. Each of these members has, in Max Black's terminology, *a system of associated commonplaces*. In a traditional simile both the tenor and the the vehicle share some of the associated commonplaces and the writer's function is to show the reader that they exist where he hadn't suspected them. In other words, the poet reveals similarities in what is usually considered dissimilar, and the degree of originality depends on how unsuspecting the reader is of these resemblances. By applying reason to the comparison, he can discover what the poet had seen before him. But Lautréamont does not point out similarities; he creates them against reason, he imposes them on us. He gives us an image which violates the most essential requirement of the traditional simile: resemblance. The affective result of this type of comparison is, initially, bewilder-

---

[1] I. A. Richards, *The Philosophy of Rhetoric* (New York, 1926) p. 127 : "the peculiar modification which the vehicle brings about is even more the work of their unlikenesses than of their likenesses."

[2] André Breton, first *Manifeste du surréalisme* (Paris, 1924) p. 64.

ment and mystification, but eventually, the discovery of a new reality. It is the image which showed the surrealists that, as Jean Brun has remarked, the word "comme" is a *verb* which does not mean "tel que". [3]

Because this type of comparison maintains an orthodox frame-work, i.e., the form of a simile, without a logical content, I shall call it a *formal simile,* and attempt to trace its evolution within *Les Chants de Maldoror.*

An embryonic example occurs in Chant I, but it is relatively mild:

> Tu dois être puissant: car tu as une figure plus qu'humaine, triste comme l'univers, belle comme le suicide.

(I, 13, p. 157)

To find suicide beautiful may seem either morbidly romantic, stoical, or even, when viewed in historical context, commonplace. When in *Bouvard et Pécuchet,* that great inventory of ready-made ideas, the Count of Faverges objects to the fashionable exaltation of suicide in the theater of the July monarchy, Pécuchet exclaims "Le suicide est beau! témoin Caton." [4]   In any case, there is not as yet an actually disruptive effect.

In Chant IV, however, we encounter a much stronger example:

> Toute une série d'oiseaux rapaces, amateurs de la viande d'au-trui et défenseurs de l'utilité de la poursuite, *beaux comme les squelettes qui effeuillent les panoccos de l'Arkansas,* voltigent autour de ton front comme des serviteurs soumis et agréés.

(IV, 4, p. 267)

---

[3] Jean Brun, "Le Problème de la sensation et le surréalisme" in *Le Surréalisme en 1947* (Paris, 1947) p. 90. And more recently, Marcelin Pleynet, writing specifically about the "beau comme" images "qui ont évidemment pour fonction de désamorcer toute tentative de 'métaphorisation' des *Chants,* en mettant l'accent sur l'adverbe comparatif 'comme' et sur les ambiguïtés qu'il introduit dans l'écriture. L'adverbe 'comme' est en effet une des articulations linguistiques les plus visiblement employées dans les chants, dans la mesure où il met en relief l'arbitraire de la fiction par le rapport que le lecteur entre-tient avec cette fiction, dans la mesure où, par l'adverbe 'comme' la fiction entend faire appel à une réalité ou fiction commune (au scripteur et au lecteur) intro-duisant dans le discours un corpus étranger dès lors pourtant assimilé au dis-cours, de la même façon que dès la première strophe du Chant I le lecteur se trouve assimilé au scripteur". "Les Chants de Maldoror et de Lautréamont", *Tel Quel* (Summer 1966), p. 46.

[4] *Œuvres complètes de Gustave Flaubert,* ed. Louis Conard (Paris, 1902), III, p. 188.

The image cannot be separated from the rest of the sentence because the context plays very strongly upon it. The simile occurs after an ironic epithet. The epithet is in apposition—a metaphor by *pointing formula,* in Brooke-Rose's terminology—emphatic by both position and tone. Then after this foregrounding device, but still part of the disjunction, we are given the comparison "beautiful as skeletons", an antithesis effect reinforced by the use of a rare word— *panoccos.* [5] And, the verb *effeuillent,* suggesting life, becomes startling because its subject *les squelettes* implies death. But the bewilderment of the reader continues: after the disjunction we have another comparison which, although still contrasting with the tenor, is more understandable (ferocious birds become tame servants). The rapid change in tone (frightening birds—irony—complementary adjective—sinister and fantastic vehicle—a relatively logical comparison) produces a sort of perplexity which bewilders or fascinates the reader, and the image, therefore, implants itself in his mind.

In the second stanza of Chant V, beginning with "Je voyais devant moi, un objet sur un tertre", Lautréamont tells an enigmatic tale, full of comic devices, all giving the impression that the poet is not serious, that he is putting on paper a world over which he has total control and which is not subject to literary conventions. The image itself breaks out of bounds:

> Quoiqu'il [cet être vivant] ne possédât pas un visage humain, il me paraissait beau comme les deux longs filaments tentaculiformes d'un insecte; ou plutôt, comme une inhumation précipitée; ou encore, comme la loi de la reconstitution des organes mutilés; et surtout comme un liquide éminemment putrescible !
>
> (V, 2, p. 291)

Not only has the distance between the tenor and the vehicles increased to the point of completely blurring the image (all the vehicles seeming equally impossible or arbitrary), but the connecting words—*ou plutôt, comme, ou encore, comme, et surtout, comme*— suggest that they are just as, if not more, accurate.

---

[5] The word is neither in the *Grand Larousse encyclopédique,* nor in Littré's *Dictionnaire de la langue française,* nor in Robert's *Dictionnaire alphabétique et analogique de la langue française.* In *Webster's New Twentieth Century Dictionary* (New York, 1960), I have found "panococo", a South American tree. Since we do not have the original manuscript of *Les Chants,* we can only assume that the word which appears in the Corti edition, based on the first edition of 1869, is a misspelling of " panococo ".

The vehicles alternate between fact and fantasy. The first and the third appear to be borrowings from science textbooks: one is an anatomical description, the other a biological law. But the second and the fourth vehicles are products of the imagination. Yet all four of them have affective connotations: an insect is generally considered repulsive, *inhumation précipitée* suggests rapid destruction, *organes mutilés* connotes aggression and *un liquide éminemment putrescible* sounds ironic because of the hyperbolic adverb. Since all the vehicles are juxtaposed and refer back to one single tenor, the categories of science and imagination become equalized and fused. Moreover, the aesthetic qualification which *beau* gives to the vehicles affects both their meanings and their connotations. In the case of the fantasies, the affective result is "black humor", the separation of the subject from the object. [6] In the case of the factual statements, however, it implies an impressionistic view of science, a subjective identification with the object. In the context of Lautréamont's sympathy for lice, the structure of an insect can indeed become beautiful; and if, as Bachelard remarks, the *crabe tourteau* is the privileged animal of the bestiary, because it would rather lose its claws than give up its prey, then a law which requires mutilated organs to grow back becomes worthy of admiration. [7]

The image, alternating between the objective approach to the subjective and the subjective approach to the objective, reverses the reader's normal perception of reality and reveals to him a world which has neither divisions nor restrictions.

As the story unfolds, as Lautréamont decides to clarify for us the mysterious beginning, the above type of image becomes fragmented, i.e. the tenor applies to only one vehicle. The three main characters (*le grand-duc de Virginie, le vautour des agneaux,* and *le scarabée*) withdraw from the scene. Each one is given the same kind of description in apposition, followed by the verb of withdrawal and an adverbial phrase of place. The three comparisons follow each

---

[6] Léon Pierre-Quint, *Le Comte de Lautréamont et Dieu*, pp. 100-101, defines humor as "une révolte supérieure de l'esprit", and André Breton *Anthologie de l'humour noir*, p. 13, quotes Freud who views humor as a means by which the super-ego maintains control over the ego. On a textual level, black humor is the result of a contrast between a taboo theme (incest, cannibalism, etc.) and its frivolous treatment. It is the effect, for example, when Swift, in *A Modest Proposal*, discusses child eating in terms of economics.

[7] Even a specialized reader, such as an entomologist or a photographer, would find the glorification of insects unexpected in a poetic context.

other rather closely, so that we have parallel constructions in rapid sequence, each one containing a formal simile:

> Le grand-duc de Virginie, beau comme un mémoire sur la courbe que décrit un chien en courant après son maître, s'enfonça dans les crevasses d'un couvent en ruines.
>
> (V, 2, p. 294)

> Le vautour des agneaux, beau comme la loi de l'arrêt de développement de la poitrine chez les adultes dont la propension à la croissance n'est pas en rapport avec la quantité de molécules que leur organisme s'assimile, se perdit dans les hautes couches de l'atmosphère.
>
> (V, 2, p. 294)

> Le scarabée, beau comme le tremblement des mains dans l'alcoolisme, disparaissait à l'horizon.
>
> (V, 2, p. 294)

In the first example, the vehicle is striking because it requires the mind to adjust to the arbitrary displacement of an object (*un mémoire*) into a background with which it has no logical rapport. This rearrangement of reality forces the reader to view the image in isolation, divorced from any causality. And the subjective qualification of *beau,* applying both to the concrete bird and to the created vision, endows the vehicle with an aesthetic aspect, forcing the reader to view both as equivalent values.

The second case, again, has a scientific law as vehicle. But this time, it is a negative law, dealing with a cessation of development and a disproportion. It may be surprising for the reader to discover that the growth of some matter has no connection with an increase in molecules. Seen subjectively, a law which denies such a cause and effect relationship can be as beautiful as the *vautour des agneaux.*

From the concrete level of object transposition and scientific fact, the third example shifts to abstraction. The vehicle's nominal structure and singular definite articles (*le tremblement des mains dans l'alcoolisme* rather than *les mains tremblantes d'un alcoolique*) make the statement appear as a general law, instead of a concrete and isolated case, and produces an image which is more intellectual than visual. Yet the content of the statement is not an idea but the symptom of a disease. A prosaïc, even repulsive, feature is raised to the level of an object of thought and acquires as much beauty and validity as the "scarabée". The mind is forced to rapidly accept the sudden changes in levels and categories presented by all three images, and finds that all preconceived notions are put into question.

Chant VI tells the story of the murder of Mervyn, a well brought-up young man, in the manner of the *roman noir* of Lewis and Maturin. Maldoror's prospective victim appears in the rue Vivienne, which has suddenly become deserted and petrified in anticipation of some ominous event. The description of the boy abruptly dissolves the carefully prepared sinister stage:

> Il est beau comme la rétractilité des serres des oiseaux rapaces; ou encore, comme l'incertitude des mouvements musculaires dans les plaies des parties molles de la région cervicale posté-rieure ; ou plutôt, comme ce piège à rats perpétuel, toujours retendu par l'animal pris, qui peut prendre seul des rongeurs indéfiniment, et fonctionner même caché sous la paille ; et sur-tout, comme la rencontre fortuite sur une table de dissection d'une machine à coudre et d'un parapluie !
>
> (VI, I, p. 327)

The sudden change in tone, brought about by the unexpected description and accumulation of seemingly unrelated vehicles, is per-plexing and may provoke laughter. [8] But if we read more slowly we find that the comparisons, as fantastic and arbitrary as they may appear, have emotive power and that the adjective *beau* which links them to a young man, and humanizes them, forces us to contemplate them subjectively, against our initial disbelief and unwillingness to take them seriously.

The first vehicle is, again, an anatomical fact. It is a feature of rapacious birds, the same animals which were used as tenor in a previous example of the formal simile (see above, p. 22). Bachelard has pointed out that birds are symbols for freedom in *Les Chants,* and that aggression is the leitmotif of the poem. [9] These birds, moreover, have the ability to show or hide their instruments of attack—*la rétractilité des serres*—a quality which is as desirable as the beauty of a human being. The equivalence of the two qualities is created by the nominal construction (rather than, for instance, *les*

---

8 However, I do not quite see how it could be called a *definition* of black humor. A. Fletcher, *Allegory* (Ithaca, 1964), p. 101.

9 Bachelard, *Lautréamont,* pp. 8-9 and p. 49.

serres rétractiles) of the vehicle, which makes an abstract concept out of a physical particularity.

As an anatomical structure is raised to a conceptual level, so a mental state (*l'incertitude*) becomes the attribute of a mutilated physiological formation, in the second vehicle. The concrete becomes an abstraction, while the abstraction becomes concrete. But, whereas in the previous example *le tremblement des mains dans l'alcoolisme* was intellectually conceivable, *l'incertitude des mouvements musculaires dans les plaies...* is almost impossible to imagine. This lack of intelligibility of the signified contrasts with the apparent scientific precision of the signifiers. Furthermore, the first vehicle connotes aggression while the second connotes mutilation (*les plaies des parties molles*). Thus the victim is as admirable as the attacker. The values are destroyed as soon as they are created.

The third vehicle introduces a mechanical instrument (*ce piège à rats*). A trap, even a rattrap, has connotations of treachery and deception (cf. *guet-apens*). Yet this object which represents fraudulence has positive moral qualities: it is persistent (*perpétuel*); it is tenacious to the point of becoming more admirable than the caught animal, who would be the normal recipient of our sympathy (*toujours retendu par l'animal pris*) but who appears ineffectual and foolish because of the reversal; it is stoical and heroic under the most adverse circumstances (*qui peut prendre seul des rongeurs indéfiniment et fonctionner même caché sous la paille*). Human virtues become attributes of a technological device whose function is generally regarded as despicable. We are forced to realize that our notions of good and evil simply depend on the manner of presentation.

From a humanized mechanism, the image shifts abruptly to the chance encounter of two apparently unrelated objects in an unrelated place. This last vehicle has been quoted often, usually in isolation from the context, thus losing the effect of juxtaposition to the other categories. It has influenced both surrealist poets and painters, and it is difficult, when discussing it, not to consider that everything which has been said about it, is now part of its content. Anna Balakian, paraphrasing Breton, states: "The surrealist image has to be a far-fetched chance encounter of two realities whose effect is likened to the light produced by the contact of two electrical conductors.... The greater the disparity, the more powerful the light, just as in electricity the greater the difference in potential of the two live wires

the greater the voltage.   The resulting spark of imagery is first
dazzling to the mind which subsequently accepts and appreciates its
reality." [10]   And Suzanne Bernard: "Cette machine à coudre et ce
parapluie, c'est, si l'on ose dire, le germe fécond d'où sortiront tant
de poèmes de Breton et de Benjamin Péret, tant de tableaux de
Chirico ou de Man Ray; c'est la porte ouverte aux rapprochements les
plus extravagants, à la danse fantastique des métaphores." [11]   Yet,
it seems too simple to assume that because two remote objects are
brought together, no matter how great their disparity, that they will
necessarily produce a spark and create light.   Aragon remarked, as
early as 1928, "Si vous écrivez, suivant une méthode surréaliste, de
tristes imbécillités, ce sont de tristes imbécillités. Sans excuses." [12]
The gratuitous juxtaposition of distant realities becomes a revelation
only when the poet has the genius to, consciously or unconsciously,
select objects that will produce electricity.   The abolition of the
requirement of logical resemblance in imagery, even if it opens the
door "aux rapprochements les plus extravagants ", demands a quality
which, because it is sought in darkness, is much harder to achieve. [13]

"La rencontre fortuite sur une table de dissection d'une machine
à coudre et d'un parapluie" implants itself in the mind of the reader,
excluding the other vehicles and even other "bringing together" of
realities (the *mémoire sur la courbe que décrit un chien* for instance)
because, even though it is irrational, it has the classical *je ne sais
quoi*. Since, from a psychoanalytic point of view, language is subli-
mation, it is of course possible to interpret the image as sexual sym-

---

[10] Anna Balakian, *Surrealism: The Road to the Absolute* (New York, 1959),
pp. 121-122.   And in the next chapter, discussing painting, she remarks that
"Out of it [the last vehicle] Max Ernst developed his famous formula of 'the
fortuitous meeting of distant realities' going a step further in declaring that
all such associations were to have a purely temporary status and might sur-
render at any moment to new combinations." p. 154.

[11] Suzanne Bernard, *Le Poème en Prose de Baudelaire jusqu'à nos jours*
(Paris, 1959), p. 246.

[12] Louis Aragon, *Le Traité du Style* (Paris, 1928), p. 192.

[13] Balakian, *Surrealism,* writes "The surrealists have written too much,
confused liberty with license at times, and probably made five unsatisfactory
images for every successful one.   There has been much trial and error, and
unfortunately the surrealists consider every word that falls from their pen
so sacred that they have freely published their errors." p. 136.   That is
because the surrealists were mainly concerned with their freedom of expression
and not with aesthetics.   The reader, however, can decide which images he
finds satisfactory, since the aesthetic experience will occur in his mind.

bolism: the sewing machine is a female symbol, the umbrella a male symbol. [14] But this can be said of anything. [15] If the success of a particular juxtaposition can be explained in any manner, it seems to me that it can only be done in terms of a Jungian archetype of the collective unconscious. [16] That is to say that the resulting image must evoke recognition in the mind of the reader rather than merely express the personal obsession of the writer.

An even more amplified example of the formal simile is the last one which occurs in the fourth stanza of Chant VI. This time the speaker is describing himself:

> ... et je me trouve beau ! beau comme le vice de conformation congénital des organes sexuels de l'homme, consistant dans la brièveté relative du canal de l'urètre et la division ou l'absence de sa paroi inférieure de telle sorte que ce canal s'ouvre à une distance variable du gland et au-dessus du pénis ; ou encore, comme la caroncule charnue, de forme conique, sillonnée par des rides transversales assez profondes, qui s'élève sur la base supérieure du bec du dindon ; ou plutôt, comme la vérité qui suit : ' le système des gammes, des modes et de leur enchaînement harmonique ne repose pas sur des lois naturelles invariables, mais il est, au contraire, la conséquence de principes esthétiques qui ont varié avec le développement progressif de l'humanité et qui varieront ; ' et surtout, comme une corvette cuirassée à tourelles !
>
> (VI, IV, pp. 339-340)

---

[14] See, for example, Salvador Dali's text in Nadeau, *Documents surréalistes* (Paris, 1948), pp. 248-251.

[15] S. Ferenczi, *Sex in Psychoanalysis*, trans. E. Jones (New York, 1950), p. 227 : "The derisive remark was once made against psychoanalysis, that the unconscious sees a penis in every convex object and a vagina or anus in every concave one. I find that this sentence well characterizes the facts."

[16] C. G. Jung, *Modern Man in Search of a Soul*, trans. W. S. Dell and Cary F. Baynes (New York, 1933), p. 165: "We mean by collective unconscious, a certain psychic disposition shaped by the forces of heredity; from it consciousness has developed. In the physical structure of the body we find traces of earlier stages of evolution, and we may expect the human psyche also to conform in its make-up to the law of phylogeny. It is a fact that in eclipses of consciousness—in dreams, narcotic states and cases of insanity—there come to the surface psychic products of content that show all the traits of primitive levels of psychic development. The images themselves are sometimes of such a primitive character that we might suppose them derived from ancient, esoteric teaching. Mythological themes clothed in modern dress also frequently appear. What is of particular importance for the study of literature in these manifestations of the collective unconscious is that they are compensatory to the conscious attitude. This is to say that they can bring a one-sided, abnormal,

The first vehicle is an anatomical description of the sexual organization of the human male, in the factual scientific language of a medical treatise. The statement deals with a defect: *le vice de conformation*. But the qualification of *beau* immediately creates ambiguity. The abstract nature of the word affects *le vice* and suggests its usual moral meaning. However, the attribute *de conformation* replaces the word in its physical context. Thus the two levels of meaning become instantly fused and, although both are pejorative, equally beautiful. In the larger frame-work of the whole sentence, an even more interesting transformation occurs. The subject, the speaker, contemplates an object, the human body, and finds the defect in the structure of the sexual organs beautiful. But the subject is presumably also human and has therefore the same anatomy as the object. It is a comment on himself and on the other, intrinsic and extrinsic, narcissistic in the psychoanalytic sense. As a result, the boundary which separates the subject from the object disappears, and the body is reunited with the world and itself.

From the beauty of an imperfection in the human anatomy, the development shifts to the category of ornithology. In the second vehicle *beau* applies to the *caroncule charnue* of the *dindon,* a ridiculous particularity of a bird which has absurd connotations (*être le dindon de la farce*). Yet this physical detail is raised to the level of a geometric abstraction (*de forme conique*) and becomes beautiful because it is seen as a pure form. Our own associations are denied through the integration of anatomy and abstract concepts of structure.

The third vehicle is a quotation from a music manual, a direct and overt bringing in from another context, a collage. It is a statement which denies that musical structures are governed by inexorable laws and asserts that they depend on cultural relativity. It appeals to Lautréamont because it is *la vérité*. Coming at the end of *Les Chants de Maldoror,* it takes on a connotation of self-justification and becomes both a defiance and a warning aimed at the reader. As an assertion it indicates that the poet knows what he is doing. As a vehicle in the simile, it completes the circle because it is an abstract formulation

---

or dangerous state of consciousness into equilibrium in an apparently purposive way."

I am not suggesting a Jungian interpretation, any more than a Freudian one, but I am simply trying to indicate that there must be a point of contact, somewhere, between the reader and the text, and that, since it is not logic, it must be a deeper, more primitive, level shared by both the writer and the reader.

about aesthetics, viewed aesthetically. A discourse on art becomes art. [17]

While the first three vehicles involve rather lengthy developments, reminiscent of the grand Homeric images which lose contact with the tenor, the last vehicle is short and stands out by contrast. It is also more easily conceivable since it is not unusual to find a ship beautiful. Yet it remains somewhat startling because it is a specific ship, a warship with turrets. It is used to attack and destroy. For Lautréamont it is a beautiful instrument of aggression, with the freedom of a fish while, for us, it is a cause of destruction. Moreover, the sudden return to a fairly logical comparison, in the micro-context of the sentence, is in itself unexpected. What would normally only be an original comparison, acquires a greater effect because it is in contrast with the pattern. It is as if the poet, having pulled the string of the bow very far, suddenly decides to release it. This is another way of denying absolutes. The logical comparison becomes just as valid as the illogical one.

I have tried to show that the vehicles, in these similes are not as arbitrary as a rapid reading would suggest. But the validity they acquire is due to the tenor *beau comme* which acts as *a title* and therefore conditions the emotive meaning of the statements. It was Lautréamont's discovery that it is possible to put any material after the word *comme*, and that the significance of the material depends on the label which is applied to it. Since the image which results from this type of juxtaposition is not based on logic, the reader is forced to provide his own connections and to perceive reality in a new way. As Anna Balakian says about surrealist painting, "The important thing was not the choice of object as much as the circumstances of its viewing and its location or position in relation to other things or beings." [18]

----

[17] Cf. *Poésies* II, p. 384: "Les jugements sur la poésie ont plus de valeur que la poésie. Ils sont la philosophie de la poésie. La philosophie, ainsi comprise, englobe la poésie. La poésie ne pourra pas se passer de la philosophie. La philosophie pourra se passer de la poésie."

[18] *Surrealism*, p. 145.

CHAPTER II

MULTIPLE SIMILES

Like the latter *formal similes,* the *multiple similes* propose several vehicles for one tenor, but they are less striking because the relationship between the parts of the comparison remains logical.

Thus, in the first stanza of Chant I, when the poet warns the reader that he is about to enter a dangerous territory and that, if he is an *âme timide,* he might do better to retreat:

> Ecoute bien ce que je te dis : dirige des talons en arrière et non en avant, comme les yeux d'un fils qui se détourne respectueusement de la contemplation auguste de la face maternelle ; ou, plutôt, comme un angle à perte de vue de grues frileuses méditant beaucoup, qui, pendant l'hiver, vole puissamment à travers le silence, toutes voiles tendues, vers un point déterminé de l'horizon, d'où tout à coup part un vent étrange et fort, précurseur de la tempête.
>
> (I, 1, p.9 123)

The tenor of the comparison (dirige tes talons...) is in itself a characteristic device of Lautréamont's style: the too precise, mechanical or scientific description of an action. [1] This has the effect of slowing down the motion which is being described, of breaking the momentum by introducing a disruptive element. It is the active equivalent of the close-up effect produced by an overly precise word which does not focus the picture but, rather, blurs it.

---

[1] For example: "Quelquefois, la grille d'un guichet s'élevait sur elle-même, en grinçant, *comme par l'impulsion ascendante d'une main qui violentait la nature du fer...*" (III, 5, pp. 237-238); "*Tes nerfs olfactifs sont enfin ébranlés par la perception d'atomes aromatiques*: ceux-ci s'élèvent de la cité anéantie, quoique je n'aie pas besoin de te l'apprendre..." (IV, 5, p. 270); "Qu'il arrive, ce jour fatal où je m'endormirai! Au réveil *mon rasoir, se frayant un passage à travers le cou,* prouvera que rien n'était, en effet, plus réel." (V, 3, p. 298); I have counted seventy-seven examples of this device.

The first vehicle compares the reading of *Les Chants* to looking, in awe, at a mother's face. This is likely to strike the reader as disproportionate: the act of beginning a book, even in anticipation of pleasure or of annoyance, is not like the emotional experience involved in gazing at the maternal countenance. And the hyperbolic vocabulary in the vehicle, (*respectueusement, la contemplation auguste, la face maternelle*) gives the gesture *qui se détourne* an aspect of theatricality. Because the statement seems mock-sentimental the effect is ironic. [2] The second vehicle moves to the abstract level of geometry, creating the same juxtaposition of categories which is so remarkable in the *formal similes*. Within the vehicle, striking changes in perspective occur: it is the angle which is vigorously flying toward a determined point on the horizon, while the cranes are meditating and appear weak because of the adjective *frileuses*. But the comparison is not complete at the end of the sentence; it is incomprehensible until we come to the verb which makes the analogy possible: "elle [the crane] vire avec flexibilité..." (p. 124) which is seventeen lines further down, and till the comparison between the reader at the beginning of the stanza and the cranes becomes clear in the very last sentence of that stanza: "elle prend ainsi un autre chemin philosophique et plus sûr" (p. 124). And the *chemin philosophique* here echoes the *chemin sauvage et abrupt* (p. 123) on which the reader is about to set out. So that, although the analogy is quite exact, its effect is weakened by the distance, the reader having lost sight of the point of departure. The first vehicle had a logical relationship to the tenor and we therefore expect the second vehicle to be as logical and perhaps more exact since *où, plutôt, comme* indicate a desire for more precision on the author's part. This expectation is denied, however, because the comparison appears, initially, to be irrelevant and therefore enigmatic. The lack of logic gives the impression that we are reading a non-sensical development. But this assumption is destroyed by the sudden revelation of the logic of the simile. Yet, the explication does not totally dispel the first impression of mystification, and even after re-reading the uneasiness does not disappear completely. The second vehicle already reveals the evolution from darkness to light which Blanchot ascribes to the whole work: "... de l'implicite à

---

[2] I use the word *irony* in Cleanth Brooks' sense, as "a general term for the kind of qualification which the various elements in a context receive from the context." *The Well Wrought* Urn (New York, 1947), p. 191.

l'explicite, de l'obscurité d'un secret à la claire conscience de l'obscurité, puis à la clarté de la révélation où pourtant l'obscur demeure..." [3]

The *multiple simile* acts as a pivot around which the stanza
revolves. The tenor and the first vehicle belong to the human and
literal level of the *lecteur* at the beginning of the poem. The second
vehicles makes the symbolic voyage of the reader concrete by transposing it onto the level of the flight of the cranes, which we see on
the abstract, although dynamic, level of geometry (l'angle qui vole).
The metaphoric *chemin* at the beginning becomes concrete through
sauvage and *abrupt,* while the literal *chemin* at the end becomes
abstract because of *philosophique.* And the ironic tone of the first
vehicle finds its counterpart in the humorous parenthetical remark in
the description: "(car, c'est elle, [the first crane], qui a le privilège
de montrer les plumes de sa queue aux autres grues inférieures en
intelligence)", and when Lautréamont comments that the crane is not
stupid, he underlines ironically the comparison between the reader
who is an *âme timide* because he turns away from the book and
behaves like a *grue.*

Lautréamont says, in the very first sentence, that the reader must
become *momentanément féroce comme ce qu'il lit* and that he must
bring to the text *une logique rigoureuse et une tension d'esprit égale
au moins à sa défiance.* Such an effort is required because the first
vehicle of the simile places the work, as Pleynet indicates, on the side
of the taboo. [4] In other words, the reader is being asked to subject
himself, through the text, to the experience of the forbidden, to a
cultural reversal. Yet, the ironic tone with which Lautréamont introduces his theme, clearly shows that he is aware that reading incest is

---

[3] Maurice Blanchot, *Lautréamont et Sade* (Paris, 1963), pp. 336-337.
[4] Giving a Freudian interpretation to *la face maternelle,* Marcelin Pleynet
says: "Comment dire plus précisément, et dès le commencement, l'étonnant
rapport que l'auteur entend entretenir avec sa langue, sa culture, son histoire,
avec ce qui, de sa langue, de sa culture, de son histoire, ne fut jamais vécu,
j'entends bien: l'inceste? C'est dans la mesure où dès son commencement,
Lautréamont affronte son savoir comme étrangeté absolue ; dans la mesure où
il rompt cette frontière du savoir qu'est le tabou, l'interdit (l'interdit, et cet
interdit majeur qu'est l'inceste); dans la mesure où il fait du fondement obscur
de la société un problème personnel, et où il interroge ce qui ne doit jamais
apparaître comme question, ce que déjà la question transgresse; c'est dans
cette mesure que Lautréamont entre dans cet espace des limites où, le nom
du père (le nom propre, ici aussi bien la distinction auteur-lecteur) se trouvant
mis entre parenthèses, l'absence de nom propre (la face maternelle) précipite
la réalité de ce qui, n'ayant pas de nom, s'écrit dans les noms, ne se vit
que dans la scription (obscure et éclairante) des noms. " *Lautréamont par
lui-même,* pp. 117-118.

not quite the same as committing it, that its projection on the written page automatically weakens its impact, enabling some people to savor *ce fruit amer sans danger*.

The second vehicle illustrates, in form and content, the fundamental problem in communication that such an experience raises: the reader brings to the book a linear perception of reality just as the cranes, although in triangular formation, fly directly toward a determined point on the horizon. At this point in the development, there is only an anticipation of the storm ahead and a warning about the danger and the difficulty in proceeding. As the poet continues, however, and as we follow him with the necessary *logique rigoureuse,* there is a realization, in Chant V, that the experience demands a circular composition (the flight of the starlings). It is precisely at this moment of realization that the plagiarisms appear in the text since it is the text itself, and not some narcissistic individual, which is the center of the circle and incorporates the world around it. As a consequence of the initial cultural reversal, the reader will have to accept being subjected to all the other resulting reversals: in the perception of reality, in moral and aesthetic values, in the manner of composition (which will have to be inclusive, discontinuous and circular rather than exclusive, continuous and linear) and in his own authorship of what he is reading (since the book has no subject but itself, the reader having become *comme ce qu'il lit*). In short, the simile is the center of the introductory stanza which contains, in microcosm, all the elements characteristic of the complete work and conveys to the reader an idea of what he may expect to encounter on the philosophical path he is about to follow.

Lautréamont had warned the reader that what he was going to read would be *féroce*. This fierceness finds expression in the eighth stanza, the one about the raging dogs. The dogs bark because they long for infinity: "Lorsque tu seras dans ton lit, que tu entendras les aboiements des chiens dans la campagne, cache-toi, ne tourne pas en dérision ce qu'ils font: ils ont soif insatiable de l'infini [*sic*], comme toi, comme moi, comme le reste des humains, à la figure pâle et longue" (p. 134). Barking is the expression of the freedom instinct in dogs which survives in human beings in the form of an outcry, whenever protestation becomes a condition for survival:

> ... les chiens... se mettent à aboyer, tour à tour, soit comme un enfant qui crie de faim, soit comme un chat blessé au ventre au-dessus d'un toit, soit comme une femme qui va enfanter,

soit comme un moribond atteint de la peste, soit comme une
jeune fille qui chante un air sublime....

(I, 8, p. 132)

The *multiple simile* is here an illustration for "comme toi, comme
moi, comme le reste des humains, à la figure pâle et longue". However, in the text this explanation does not precede the image, as above,
but is given two pages later, so that the reader is, once more, first
mystified, then enlightened. [5] The alternation of adjectival and par-
ticipal adjective clauses, anaphorically introduced, creates a pattern
which is in contrast with the outcry theme. The last vehicle, by its
juxtaposition to the others, makes *chanter un air sublime* the equivalent of *aboyer* and *crier,* so that the rhythm created by the regularity
of the syntactical structure becomes a reflection of that same inter-
changeability. This is emphasized by the repeated use of the connecting tool words (*soit comme*) which suggests arbitrariness. In
other words, the image represents the underlying theme of *Les Chants
de Maldoror*: the poet's song is a cry of protest.

One of the primary means of rebelling, of breaking loose, is the
ability to become something else, something quicker or more powerful. This metamorphosis is usually accomplished very rapidly, without
introductory comment, forcing the reader to accept the changes in
form while they are occurring. In the same eighth stanza, however,
the *multiple simile* anticipates Maldoror's transformations:

Nul n'a encore vu les rides vertes de mon front ; ni les os en
saillie de ma figure maigre, pareille aux arêtes de quelque grand
poisson, ou aux rochers couvrant les rivages de la mer, ou aux
abruptes montagnes alpestres que je parcourus souvent, quand
j'avais sur ma tête des cheveux d'une autre couleur.

(I, 8, p. 134)

Since he had said before that he did not like what he was (*Je
suis le fils de l'homme et de la femme, d'après ce qu'on m'a dit. Ça
m'étonne... je croyais être davantage !*) and that he would rather have
been *le fils de la femelle du requin,* each vehicle of the simile offers

---

[5] See Yvonne Rispal, "Le Monde de Lautréamont à travers l'étude du langage." *Cahiers du Groupe Françoise Minkowska,* October 1962. Although this
study tries primarily to interpret the poem as a Rorschach test, and to penetrate the author's personality by means of the text, it makes some comments
which are interesting from a literary point of view: Lautréamont's tendency
to invert is a manifestation of his duality, but " ... le renversement devient un
mode de vision, de perception." (p. 15.)

the possibility of taking advantage of the various attributes of other physical forms, from the bigness of a fish to the abruptness of alpine mountains.   In this context, then, in which the similarity between the hero's aspect and other forms of nature is suggested, the end of the sentence ("quand j'avais sur ma tête des cheveux d'une autre couleur") makes the phenomenon of metamorphosis an experienced reality. The reader is caught by surprise because of what seems to be a simple explanation of the last vehicle, but is, in fact, a continuation of the descriptive tenor: Maldoror's frightening appearance. The superfluous detail *sur ma tête,* putting into question, by implication, what the reader would normally take for granted, further enhances the impression of a lack of formal physical restrictions.   Moreover, the vehicles do not give us a clearer picture of Maldoror's appearance: it is difficult to visualize salient facial bones which are like fishbones, rocks or alpine mountains. The statement remains enigmatic. It is a truism that in the act of communication, the fewer the given details, the greater the need for audience participation. In an enigma, as in a detective story, the lack of clues forces the reader to become involved in the development.

In the examples we have just seen, the several vehicles are given as alternatives, seeming to indicate a high degree of freedom of choice.   In the following examples, the vehicles are accumulated, either by a simple conjunction or asyndetically, to underline the polymorphous quality of the tenor.

The narrator has been watching a human being, swimming in the sea, with a fin, and duck paws instead of arms and legs. Lautréamont, having stated that this was "un monstre, qui s'est approprié les marques distinctives de la famille des palmipèdes" catches himself and thinks better of it:

> Qui parle ici d'appropriation ? Que l'on sache bien que l'homme par sa nature multiple et complexe, n'ignore pas les moyens d'en élargir encore les frontières ; il vit dans l'eau, comme l'hippocampe ; à travers les couches supérieures de l'air, comme l'orfraie ; et sous la terre comme la taupe, le cloporte et la sublimité du vermisseau.
>
> (IV, 7, p. 276)

Each vehicles has a different *ground,* i.e. illustrates a particular ability of man, but the image is the result of the juxtaposition of all three vehicles to the one tenor.   Usually, when we want to indicate man's versatility, we speak in general terms: man can swim like a

fish, fly like a bird, etc. Lautréamont, however, chooses to use the
species, rather than the genus. This precision obscures, rather than
clarifies, the reader's vision and limits his imagination by imposing
on it specific animals. When the idea is couched in generalities,
man's greatness and superiority are implied. By being so precise,
Lautréamont makes man appear as a ridiculous creature. The animals
are not the privileged ones of the bestiary; they are not used by
Maldoror for his aggressive metamorphoses since they have no power
to attack. [6] Their connotations are rather unflattering: the sea-horse
is an absurd, bastard form which stands out as an anachronism in its
environment, the *orfraie* is a rapacious bird, *taupe* suggests near-
sightedness, *cloporte* has associations of hiding is darkness and of
humidity, and *vermisseau* is used figuratively for a miserable and frail
being. The apparent objective scientific precision of the literal level
becomes fused with the derogatory and subjective implications of
the figurative level. Moreover, the concreteness of the specific animals
suddenly evaporates into abstraction when we come to the nominal
structure of *la sublimité du vermisseau* which transforms the physical
insect into a concept and endows it with an unexpected aesthetic
value. The simile becomes an instrument of attack which mocks man
by ridiculing him and confuses the reader by merging the literal and
the concrete with the figurative and the abstract, the subjective with
the objective.

But the *multiple simile* can also be a means of glorification. The
poet addresses the ocean:

> Ta grandeur morale, image de l'infini, est immense comme la
> réflexion du philosophe, comme l'amour de la femme, comme la
> beauté divine de l'oiseau, comme les méditations du poète.
>
> (I, 9, p. 141)

The humanizing attribute of the tenor (*grandeur morale*) creates
an initial disruptive effect since the metaphor in apposition (*image
de l'infini*) and the adjectival link (*immense comme*) are descriptive
of the concrete ocean, rather than of its abstract attribution. We are
prepared to view the ocean as immense and as the image of the
infinite. It would then be a visual representation of all the humanistic
values expressed in the vehicles. The categories would merely sym-
bolyze man's aspirations. Being humanized and abstracted, however,
the ocean is put on the same level as the vehicles which are abstract

---

[6] See Chapter IV, below.

by virtue of the definite articles.   In this way, the tenor is no longer
just representative, but becomes the embodiment of all the honorific
vehicles.   The moral grandeur of the ocean contains man's thought,
love, beauty, poetic contemplation. Furthermore, the asyndetic structure of the sentence suggests that the enumeration is not complete,
that it could progress to infinity, that the ocean is everything. The
object transcends its form and acquires a subjective significance.

Although the *multiple simile* may, to the casual critic, seem like a
gratuitous display of virtuosity, it has a very definite function in
the texture of the poem.   Its component vehicles bring together not
only human, animal and geological categories but also reality and
imagination.   It is a major step toward the creation of a cosmic entity,
toward that unity which the surrealists tried to achieve. [7]

---

[7] Ferdinand Alquié describes the surrealist project this way: "... on aspire
à un bouleversement qui, en même temps qu'il transformerait le Monde, chan-
gerait la vie. L'espoir en un tel bouleversement suppose la parenté des puis-
sances qui construisent l'Univers et des principes qui dirigent nos pensées,
il appelle la libération des forces communes à l'homme et à la Nature, forces
dont le désir nous fournit l'image la plus approchée". *Philosophie du surréalisme* (Paris, 1955), p. 52.

CHAPTER III

THE HOMERIC ANALOGICAL EPITHET

This is the device which occurs most frequently in *Les Chants de Maldoror* (I have counted eighty-four examples of it).[1] Lautréamont's partiality to it is probably due to its particular virtues: its classical form gives the reader the security of familiarity, its conciseness favors quick, unexpected associations. The poet has relatively great flexibility of juxtaposition within a strict, traditional framework. It is a three-part structure in which the tenor is a noun and the vehicle a noun plus a noun, or a noun plus an adjective. This is, of course, the case of the usual French form of the device only. The compound form of the Greek is more easily assimilated into English. M. de Rochefort in his *Discours sur Homère,* which precedes his translation of 1772 says: "Veut-on rendre un mot composé? Ce mot qui passe rapidement dans la diction de l'original, ne fait plus que se traîner dans nos périphrases." and in the translation he writes "Avec ses doigts de rose, / l'Aurore vint ouvrir les portes du soleil."; but in P. Giguet's version we find the normal French form: "l'aurore aux doigts de rose" (Revised edition, 1866) p. 12. In English, however, the translations are "rosy-fingred Morning" (Spenser) or "rosy-fingered morn" (Pope). [2] The French reader is, therefore, likely to bring to Lautréamont the Giguet form of the Homeric epithet as a

---

[1] It is simply the traditional Homeric epithet which is analogical, and produces an image, when the vehicle (or one of its parts) introduces a semantic category different from that in the tenor.

[2] See Brooke-Rose, *Grammar,* p. 171 and note. She points out that neither the English nor the French form represents exactly the original since English has to verbalize the noun. The *ed* ending is the equivalent of the French particle. But, it seems to me, there is an affective difference. The English form loses its distinctiveness as a classical epithet; it becomes just another "pure attribute" metaphor (Brooke-Rose) while the French form remains easily recognizable, even if the reader is not aware of its Greek origin. Thus "the white-haired revolver" may well be a striking personification, but it lacks the contrast between the traditional form and the novelty of the association which "le révolver à cheveux blancs" has.

frame of reference. [3] The originality of this type of image, then, depends on the extent to which it varies in content, or in combination of parts, from what the reader's culture makes him anticipate, i.e. from such epithets as "Junon, déesse aux bras blancs" (p. 2), "les Grecs aux yeux vifs" (p. 5), "les Grecs à la belle chevelure" (p. 10), etc.... This does not mean that Homer's epithets are neutral or uninteresting, that they do not have degrees of affectivity in their own context, but that the reader brings to *Les Chants* the experience of the classical device, which we can therefore consider as *degré zéro*. In the context of the *Iliad,* for instance, "La mer aux bruits tumultueux" (p. 2) is certainly a striking image since the adjective *tumultueux* applies not only to the noise of the sea, but also to its aspect, and this produces an interweaving of the auditory and visual perceptions. Yet this image can become, in turn, the neutral level of "Vieil océan, aux vagues de cristal" (I, 9, p. 136) which is striking because the elements are juxtaposed: the waves become stagnant and solid, and crystal becomes fluid and mobile. I do not mean to compare Lautréamont's epithets to Homer's but simply to emphasize that they must be seen in the light of the reader's habits and expectations. [4]

Since the degree of intensity depends on the distance between the familiarity of the form and the unfamiliarity of the content, I have thought it best to classify Lautréamont's Homeric epithets by order of disruptive effect. It has been pointed out that Lautréamont seems to despise adjectives for their weakness and to prefer nouns. [5] This becomes quite apparent when we compare the pejorative connotation of the adjectival form of a word with the flattering connotation of the nominal form of the same word. For example: "Arrière, malfaiteur, à la tête *échevelée* (p. 332) but "O adolescent, aux *cheveux* blonds, aux yeux si doux..." (p. 130), and, although le *pou* is venerated in *Les Chants* (see II, 9, pp. 185-190) "... *de magnifiques poux, ornés d'une beauté remarquable, monstres à l'allure de sage*"

---

[3] This has so become the norm that Marc Eigeldinger, *L'évolution dynamique de l'image au dix-neuvième siècle* (Neuchâtel, 1943), considers that some of these epithets "pouraient passer pour des traductions presque littérales d'Homère." (p. 235.)

[4] See M. Riffaterre, *Le Style des Pléiades de Gobineau* (New York, 1957, p. 59 n. 2: "il (le degré zéro) peut être absolu, comme c'est le cas pour le contexte atone [a context which is not at variance with the linguistic norm]; il peut être relatif, c'est-à-dire qu'un fait de style expressif est parfois le point de départ d'un autre par rapport auquel il joue le rôle de degré zéro... "

[5] Bachelard, *Lautréamont*, pp. 58-59 and Rispal "Le monde de Lautréamont", p. 27.

(pp. 185-186), the adjective is nonetheless downgrading: "l'homme, à la chevelure *pouilleuse*..." (p. 213).

I have therefore divided my examples into two main categories: 1) those in which the vehicle is modified by an adjective and 2) those in which it is modified by another noun. Within each category, the examples are arranged by order of progression from neutral to highest relief. This classification is not intended to be absolute; some of the examples, specially borderline cases, are certainly open to question. I have, however, tried to keep the gradation as objective as possible.

1) An adjective as modifier.

a) the adjective, although pejorative, is not unexpected:

... les hommes, aux épaules étroites...

(I, 5, p. 126)

... les hommes, à l'aspect brutal...

(I, 9, p. 142)

Un de ces hommes, à l'œil froid...

(II, 2, p. 168)

Disparais le plus tôt possible loin de moi, coupable à la face blême !

(V, 4, p. 299)

b) the adjective is not disruptive by itself but a double vehicle calls attention to the whole structure:

O adolescent, aux cheveux blonds, aux yeux si doux...

(I, 6, p. 130)

J'ai vu les hommes à la tête laide et aux yeux terribles enfoncés dans l'orbite obscur...

(1, 5, p. 126)

In the second example, the adjective *laide* is derogatory by definition and not, like *étroites, froid,* or *blême,* by association, and in the second vehicle the noun has two adjectives (both pejorative in the context) and an adverb of place, modified by a pejorative adjective. The accumulation of derogatory attributes and the relatively ample structure make this image much more striking than any we have thus far seen.

c) the adjective becomes striking because of the noun which it modifies:

> ... la grande tombe, à la figure vieille.
>
> (I, 6, p. 130)
>
> Ecoutez les pensées de mon enfance, quand je me réveillais, humains, à la verge rouge...
>
> (II, 12, p. 200)
>
> ... l'homme, à la salive saumâtre...
>
> (II, 13, p. 210)

In the first example, *vieille,* by its postposition, reinforces the unusual personification of the tomb. In the second case, the anatomical sexual detail used insultingly is striking by itself, but the image is also unexpected because it refers to the lower part of the body, which is extremely rare in Lautréamont's epithets. They usually apply to hair, face, eyes, lips, shoulders, etc. While Homer may give us features like "Agamemnon, au loin [*sic*] puissant" (Giguet, p. 3), "Thétis, aux pieds d'argent" (p. 13), and "Iris, aux pieds rapides comme les vents" (p. 33), I have found only one other example in Lautréamont ("le crime, à la patte sombre") and that is in an animalization of an abstraction. Moreover, color adjectives are relatively rare in Lautréamont and they have generally unpleasant connotations: "Nul n'a encore vu les rides *vertes* de mon front" (p. 134), "... l'on voit, plongé dans d'amères réflexions, toutes les choses revêtir des formes *jaunes,* indécises, fantastiques" (p. 132), "... mon vaste corps, pareil à un nuage *noirâtre*" (p. 143). [6] The third example is remarkable because an adjective with the depreciative suffix "âtre" modifies a noun with repulsive connotations "salive". I consider it somewhat stronger than the previous case, for it is self-descriptive (*l'homme* being Maldoror) and therefore less expected than it would be in an attack on humanity.

d) the adjective is striking enough to affect the noun:

> Arrière, malfaiteur, à la tête échevelée.
>
> (VI, II, p. 332)
>
> ... les papillons, aux zigzags agaçants
>
> (III, 2, p. 228)
>
> ... l'homme, à la chevelure pouilleuse
>
> (II, 15, p. 213)

---

[6] It is notable how different Lautréamont's attitude toward colors is from Rimbaud's. On the possible influence of the former on the latter, see Francis J. Carmody, "A Correlation of the Chronology and Lexicon of Rimbaud's Verse," *FR,* XXXIII (January 1960), 247-256.

In the first example, the adjective reinforces the insult of the tenor. The second case represents a typical Lautréamont reversal. It has been noted that in *Les Chants* all our concepts are reversed. The ugly becomes beautiful, good becomes evil, small becomes enormous, the inanimate becomes animate, etc. [7] And since generally repulsive insects such as lice become sacred, likable butterflies become annoying. Furthermore, the pejorative impression of the epithet clashes with the pleasing sound, increasing the disruptive effect. But while, here, the adjective shares the emphasis with an unusual and onomatopoetic noun (the feature being a motion rather than a physical characteristic), in the last example the focus is completely on the adjective. The word is striking by itself, and is definitely used insultingly, since it is in the stanza where Man is pursued by his conscience, and Maldoror, after attempting to defend him, gives up the task as being quite impossible. Yet, the word occurs at the beginning of stanza 15, only six strophes after the lice panegyric, so that its meaning is ambiguous. Is it an insult or is it merely a description? The reader's reaction to it has been blunted by the weakening of its connotations. [8] Paradoxically, since the adjective does not have its normal power, the stylistic effect has become greater: the reader can rely neither on the notions he brings to the work, nor on those he acquires while reading it.

e) the adjective is disruptive:

> ... la mare où, recouvert de brouillard, bleuit et mugit le crime, à la patte sombre !
>
> (III, 5, p. 247)

> O pou, à la prunelle recroquevillée...
>
> (II, 9, p. 187)

> Sur ma nuque, comme sur un fumier, pousse un énorme champignon, aux pédoncules ombellifères.
>
> (IV, 4, p. 264)

The adjective is, of course, not the only remarkable thing about the first and last images. If the first example read *la mare où, le crime, à la patte sombre, bleuit et mugit, recouvert de brouillard* we

---

[7] See Rispal, "Le Monde de Lautréamont," pp. 15-16.
[8] The predominant view of lice is best expressed in this comment from the article *pou* in the *Larousse du XIX siècle*: "C'est l'insecte honteux pour ceux qui se respectent et dont on évite de prononcer le nom vulgaire en bonne compagnie."

would simply have an animalization of an abstract noun—crime is an animal which, protected by fog, roars in a stagnant pool—a not unusual allegorical device. The postposition of the subject creates, at first, a confusion of human and animal categories: *bleuir,* although it has connotations of decay and could therefore refer to any living matter, is an essentially human characteristic (*bleuir de froid*), while *mugir* is an almost dead metaphor, commonly used for persons. But this initial reaction is upset by the vehicle of the Homeric epithet which, through the word *patte,* puts the image in the animal category. Then, by the use of the adjective *sombre,* rather than of a more concrete color, we are brought back to the abstract level of the tenor *le crime.* We go from the human and animal *bleuit et mugit* to the abstract *le crime* to the animal *patte* to the possibly abstract *sombre.* I say "possibly", because at that point we can no longer be sure whether *sombre* is to be taken literally as a description for *patte,* meaning "of a dark color" or whether it applies figuratively to *le crime.* This mystification of the reader is, however, not gratuitous. Crime is *recouvert de brouillard,* both literally, in this context, and metaphorically. Its outline cannot be perceived clearly, it can take, or partake of, all forms, and the structure of the image expresses the undefinable quality of the concept, i.e., the aspect of a monster.

In the second example, *prunelle* is a somewhat more precise detail than one would normally expect in a Homeric epithet. We are accustomed to *les yeux,* or *l'œil* or *le regard* but *prunelle* gives a close-up effect, which in the context of the lice eulogy, unsettles the reader. Although it is a scientific fact that the eye of a louse is very small, the adjective *recroquevillée* does not have the emotive neutrality of a scientific statement. It has, on the contrary, a connotation of ridicule and its use in an invocation is disconcerting. Here, the effect is produced by a mocking, slightly colloquial, word in a pattern which made the reader expect a flattering, or, at least, a factual word.

An even greater disruption is achieved in the next example, by reversing the process. An extremely repulsive image suddenly loses its momentum and stops short because the vehicle in the Homeric epithet is so purely scientific that it is incomprehensible without a dictionary. Yet *pédoncules ombellifères,* bewildering as it may be on the semantic level, is pleasing on the phonetic level and is cast in a traditional poetic mold. This makes it mysterious rather than mystifying, an enigma with the surrealist quality of the *merveilleux.* By transposing the words from an encyclopedia into the image, Lautréamont has endowed them with the potential for poetic pleasure, in the Hytier sense of the expression. [9] Immediately after this affective change, however, the poet continues the repellent description of Maldoror, rendering us unable to adjust to the new note by abruptly returning us to our initial impression. Since the reader is constantly left off-balance, he loses all certitude.

2) The modifier is a descriptive noun.

   a) the noun is not unusual.

> Le corsaire, aux cheveux d'or, a reçu la réponse de Mervyn.
>
> > (VI, vii, p. 350)
>
> Une femme, à la voix de soprano...
>
> > (II, 6, p. 181)

In neither case is the noun particularly suggestive in its juxtaposition to the other parts of the simile: *cheveux d'or* has become a cliché for *cheveux blonds*, [10] and a woman with a soprano voice is not particularly remarkable. Nonetheless, the examples are not totally neutral in context. The first refers to Maldoror who is not often described in attractive terms. We are likely to think of *pirate* rather than of *corsaire* which, in Max Black's terminology, [11] has a romantic *system of associated commonplaces*. But we can accept the fact that

---

[9] See Jean Hytier, *Le Plaisir poétique* (Paris, 1923) and "L'Activité Poétique et l'Activité Esthétique dans la Poésie" in *Les Arts de littérature* (Paris, 1945), pp. 11-48.
Poetic pleasure differs from aesthetic pleasure in that it exacts only the feeling and the play of images around an affective theme. "Le plaisir poétique est un jeu d'images librement systématisées pour la satisfaction de l'affectivité profonde." *Les Arts de littérature*, p. 19. It can be found almost everywhere "sous condition d'être organisé par le sentiment", *ibid.*, p. 18. Lautréamont achieves this change in affectivity by transposing a statement from a context organized by intellect into one of feeling.
[10] For the value of a cliché as a stylistic device, see Michael Riffaterre, "Fonctions du cliché dans la prose littéraire", *CAIEF*, 16 (March 1964) 81-95. The cliché is noticeable precisely because it is a cliché, and in the above example *cheveux d'or* is stricking as a unit and because it is characteristic of a poetic context (see infra, p. 49 n. 16). However, *d'or* is not unexpected in juxtaposition to *cheveux* and does not, therefore, produce a disruptive effect.
[11] Max Black, *Models and Metaphors* (Ithaca, 1962). About the metaphor "Man is a wolf" (p. 39), Black says "What is needed is not so much that the reader shall know the standard dictionary meaning of *wolf* — or be able to use that word in literal senses — as that he shall know what I call *the system of associated commonplaces*" (p. 40), that is, the range of connotations of a word.

Maldoror has made himself alluring in order to seduce Mervyn. The second example is used to emphasize the protagonist's inability to appreciate any product of humanity, even a beautiful voice; all he hears is *le tocsin de la cannonade*. In the antithesis, then, *soprano*, meaning "very beautiful", is a hyperbole and has ironic connotations.

b) the modifying noun produces a metaphor.

> O poulpe, au regard de soie... [12]
>
> (I, 9, p. 136)
>
> ... de magnifiques poux, ornés d'une beauté remarquable, monstres à l'allure de sage.
>
> (II, 9, pp. 185-186)

In the first example, Maldoror invokes an animal which represents evil and establishes a strong identification with it: "toi, dont l'âme est inséparable de la mienne..." Although *poulpe* is a standard symbol for evil in the reader's mind, [13] it is a privileged creature in the animal world of *Les Chants,* because of its tentacles. [14] It is by means of the word *soie* that Lautréamont upgrades the octopus, that he crosses the distance between the two concepts of the animal. For the reader *poulpe* has unpleasant connotations, and *soie* pleasant ones, but because of the juxtaposition, both systems of associations become intermingled and *soie* takes on some of the repulsive attributes of *poulpe.*

A similar process occurs in the second example: *Le pou,* as we have seen before, is another highly regarded animal in Lautréamont's bestiary. [15] But here the buildup is somewhat more complex. First we have the flattering preceding adjective, then the tenor *poux,* then a very complimentary description in apposition, then the vehicle *monstres,* which suddenly transforms the beautiful small insects into frightening gigantic creatures (since *monstres* suggests bigness). However, *monstres* is itself the tenor of the Homeric epithet, whose vehicle gives the monsters the appearance of wise men. None of the

---

[12] This image does not appear until the 1869 edition. The 1868 edition of Chant I had "Ah! Dazet toi dont l'âme..." and the version which appeared in *Parfum de l'âme*, a Bordeaux review, had "Ah! D... toi dont l'âme..." Georges Dazet was a school friend of Lautréamont, and one of the dedicatees of *Poésies*.

[13] In Henry Morier's *Dictionnaire de poétique et de rhétorique* (Paris, 1961), p. 429, "poulpe" is listed under "symboles consacrés ou conventionnels" as "incarnation du mal (depuis Hugo et *Les Travailleurs de la Mer*)."

[14] See Bachelard, pp. 41-42.

[15] *Ibid.*, pp. 38-39.

forms or qualities remain static and the reader's mind has to accept the rapid changes without any logical explanations and to adapt to a new reality, a world in which lice are beautiful monsters who look like wise men. Because the reader's prejudices remain constant throughout, the text creates an effect of continual contrast.

But in neither example is there an actual metamorphosis produced by the vehicle of the Homeric analogy: *regard* and *allure* are both not concrete enough while *soie* and *sage* are too rich in associations. When the noun is more concrete and the modifier more limited in its suggestive power, the vehicle is likely to be taken literally and the metaphor becomes a metamorphosis.

c) the modifying noun achieves a metamorphosis.

L'homme, aux lèvres de bronze...	(II, 14, p. 212) and (VI, V, p. 346)
L'homme, à la prunelle de jaspe...	(II, 14, p. 213)
L'homme, aux lèvres de jaspe...	(VI, VI, p. 346)
L'homme, aux lèvres de saphir...	(VI, VI, p. 349)
L'homme, aux lèvres de soufre...	(VI, VIII, p. 354)

In all these examples *l'homme* refers to Maldoror. The first image occurs twice (p. 212 and p. 346) and is in both cases followed by the *jaspe* image. The first set ("L'homme, aux lèvres de bronze" and "l'homme, à la prunelle de jaspe...") is in Chant II, pp. 211-213, in the stanza where Maldoror resuscitates the young man who had tried to commit suicide by throwing himself into the Seine. It is the protagonist's only good deed in the book. Here, the features are different but in the examples from Chant VI, they are all *lèvres,* and only the material of the modifier changes from metal (*bronze*) to precious stones (*saphir* and *jaspe*) to chemical (*soufre*). The usual materials found in Homeric epithets are gold, silver or stone, all rich in connotations. Lautréamont's choice ranges from the fairly common and fertile *bronze* to the almost unsuggestive *soufre*. [16] His modifiers may

---

[16] The list of figurative uses for *or, bronze, saphir, jaspe,* and *soufre* in the *Larousse du XIXe siècle* requires several pages for gold, including this example from Régnier: "L'Aurore, aux cheveux d'or, au visage de roses / Déjà comme à demi découvrait toutes choses", while bronze only has a few columns with Alexandre Dumas, père's "Alors, l'homme de bronze sentit son cœur se dilater dans sa poitrine." There is one example for *saphir* and none for either *jaspe* or *soufre*.

bring to mind certain qualities, such as hardness, certain textures or colors, but they do not have the symbolic value of gold and silver. This limitation of connotative possibilities is what differentiates a metamorphosis from a metaphor. In a metaphor, at least one word has to be used figuratively, or open to figurative interpretations. A metamorphosis occurs when all the words of an image are so restricted in their associations that they must be taken literally, forcing the reader to accept imagination as reality. Furthermore, in the context of *Les Chants'* rapid form changes, [17] we can readily believe that Maldoror's lips and eyes become petrified by certain elements which, in turn, become animalized by their contact with living matter. [18] But the features, although solidified, do not remain unchanged. The last four "lip" examples are found relatively close to each other, between pages 346 and 354, so that the substance alters rapidly, both in material and in quality (from bronze to sulphur). This underlines the protagonist's ability to transform himself and prevents the reader from acquiring a definite picture of his appearance.

d) the modifying noun is a degrader.

L'homme, à la figure de crapaud...

(II, 1, p. 161)

Ainsi donc, horrible Eternel, à la figure de vipère...

(II, 2, p. 164)

L'abrutissement, au groin de porc, le [Dieu] couvrait de ses ailes protectrices, et lui jetait un regard amoureux.

(III, 4, p. 235)

Je le voyais maintenant, l'homme, à l'encéphale dépourvu de protubérance annulaire !

(V, 2, p. 290)

---

[17] Lautréamont explicitly states the desirability of metamorphosis: "La métamorphose ne parut jamais à mes yeux que comme le haut et magnanime retentissement d'un bonheur parfait, que j'attendais depuis longtemps. Il était enfin venu le jour où je fus un pourceau !" (p. 274) The instances of form changes are frequent: "Quel ne fut pas son étonnement, quand il vit Maldoror, changé en poulpe, avancer contre son corps ses huit pattes monstrueuses, dont chacune, lanière solide, aurait pu embrasser facilement la circonférence d'une planète" (pp. 215-216), "Ils [les cris] se changèrent en vipères, en sortant par sa bouche, et allèrent se cacher dans les brousailles..." (p. 215), and at the beginning of stanza VI, Chant VI, in which three of the examples under discussion are located, "Pour ne pas être reconnu, l'archange avait pris la forme d'un crabe tourteau, grand comme une vigogne" (p. 346). Bachelard, *Lautréamont*, p. 22 has pointed out the rapidity of these métamorphoses: "En effet, chez Lautréamont, la métamorphose est urgente et directe: elle se réalise un peu plus vite qu'elle n'est pensée; le sujet, étonné, voit soudain qu'il a construit un objet."

[18] On the senses, their organs, and respective values in Lautréamont, see Rispal, "Le monde de Lautréamont", pp. 35-37.

Here, the Homeric epithet is a weapon against Maldoror's two enemies: Man and God. *L'homme* in the first and last examples refers to humanity. The animals involved are not among the privileged creatures of *Les Chants*. Neither the toad nor the pig has any power to attack, and the viper symbolizes perfidy rather than cruelty. [19] In the structure of the analogy, they are relegated to the modifier of the vehicle, [20] while the louse and the octopus are the tenor of other comparisons. This does not mean that the vehicle is the weaker part of the image; clearly, in the above examples, the modifier is the explosive element, the one that attracts the reader's attention. But in the previous *pou* and *poulpe* similes, the tenor, aided by the invocation or the honorific adjective, creates the original disruptive effect, which is then reinforced by the vehicle. While the more favored animals have attributes of their own, the less favored ones are used as insulting modifiers. When the animal is in the tenor, the device works against the reader's normal associations, but when they are in the vehicle, the connotations in the reader's mind are used to degrade the tenor. Still, as in other examples of the device, there is a contamination of forms: Man and God acquire animal attributes and animals become human and godlike.

The third case represents a higher degree of complexity than the first two. The tenor (a derogatory abstract noun) has three vehicles from three different species:

a) the Homeric epithet animalizes the abstraction by the attribution of a pig feature ("*groin de porc*"). The attribution is made more emphatic by the use of a precise word *groin* rather than *figure*.

b) the second vehicle endows the pig with wings, through the cliché *ailes protectrices*. The cliché is taken literally here, because the previous vehicle had put the image on an animal level. The idea of God as being protected by the wings of stupidity, an ironic attribution in itself, gives the description a sarcastic overtone.

---

[19] See Bachelard, p. 31.

[20] I am using the word *modifier* in M. C. Beardsley's sense: "Let us use the term 'attribution' for any linguistic expression containing at least two words, one of which denotes a class and also characterizes it in some way, and the other of which qualifies or modifies the characterization. I shall call an expression an attribution whether it is merely a phrase, 'large dogs,' or a complete sentence. 'The dogs are large' But when I require the distinction, I shall speak of 'phrase-attributions' and 'sentence-attributions'. The term that is modified in either case, 'dogs', I shall call the *subject* of the attribution; the other term, 'large', the *modifier*." *Aesthetics: Problems in the philosophy of criticism* (New York, 1958), pp. 138-139.

c) the third vehicle, endowing stupidity with human emotions, achieves a personification. *Amoureux* reinforces the ironic effect of *protectrices*.

For the idea of God's obtuseness, we are given an image in which stupidity, the subject, becomes concrete, although not in any recognizable form, shelters God, the object, and flirts with Him.

We must, of course, here, disregard the normative prejudice against mixed metaphors. The requirement that a metaphorical development be logical is the result of a concept of static forms. If, as Bachelard suggests, we open up to dynamic changes in form in order to penetrate the transformed world of *Les Chants,* then, the very idea of mixed metaphors disappears, since forms will partake of one another. [21]

The fourth example is similar to the *énorme champignon, aux pédoncules ombellifères,* in the sense that the attribute is a scientifically correct fact, expressed in terms that are unintelligible at first glance. But here, the anatomical description has a definite emotive tinge. First, there is an amplification, since both the noun and the modifier have adjectives. This is likely to increase the confusion of the reader. Then, the only word which can immediately be understood, *dépourvu,* has a derogatory connotation, implying that man lacks something. The impression is given that, because he does not have a feature which, presumably, other creatures have, he is ridiculous. An objective scientific statement becomes a mocking device, a means of attack. It is a weapon which works two ways: against the tenor *l'homme,* Maldoror's enemy, and, intellectually, against the reader.

We have seen some of the most striking uses which Lautréamont makes of the traditional structure. By endowing it with unexpected word combinations, he manages to create highly original images which disrupt our preconceived notions and, sometimes, rearrange reality. In their desire to change the world and life, the surrealists saw the potential of the Homeric epithet and took full advantage of it. Consider, for instance, Breton's beautiful love poem:

> Ma femme à la chevelure de feu de bois
> Aux pensées d'éclairs de chaleur
> A la taille de sablier...
> Ma femme aux tempes d'ardoise de toit de serre

---

[21] See Bachelard, p. 38.

et de buée aux vitres
Ma femme aux épaules de champagne
Et de fontaine à têtes de dauphin sous la glace...
Ma femme aux aisselles de marbre et de fênes
De la nuit de la Saint-Jean... [22]

[22] André Breton, *L'union libre* (1931), reprinted in *Poèmes* (Paris, 1948), pp. 65-67.

CHAPTER IV

ANIMAL SIMILES

For Gaston Bachelard, *Les Chants de Maldoror* are a manifestation of Lautréamont's *complexe de la vie animale* and appear therefore as a *phénoménologie de l'agression*. [1] The work is an expression of the primitive, pre-human, life instinct whose aggressive im-
pulses are uncontrolled: "Le vouloir-vivre est ici un vouloir-attaquer.
Il n'est jamais endormi, jamais défensif, jamais repu. Il s'étale dans
son hostilité essentielle. La psychologie humaine socialisée en souffre;
elle apparaît toute violentée, brutalement déformée; mais l'ardent
passé animal de nos passions ressuscite à nos yeux épouvantés. En
résumé, La Fontaine a écrit une psychologie humaine sous la fable
animale, Lautréamont a écrit une fable inhumaine en revivant les
impulsions brutales, si forte encore dans le cœur des hommes." [2]
Aggressiveness is consequently the unrepressed life-instinct, and when
Maldoror transforms himself into an animal, it is one whose instrument of attack provides immediate and gratuitous cruelty: "C'est par
le dedans que l'animalité est saisie, dans son geste atroce, irrecti-
fiable, issu d'une volonté pure." [3] The principal agents of the cruel
act are the claw and the tentacle. The claw is used mainly to scratch
and to grip, while the tentacle, with its suction cups, clings and
strangles. The animal hierarchy in *Les Chants* is based on these
means of aggression. Thus, the louse attaches itself to the human
body, and as a parasite is capable of destroying its host. The vulture
and the eagle have claws and a beak which are used to lacerate, and
wings to guarantee their freedom. The octopus, with its numerous
appendages, suffocates its victim. The shark's raison d'être seems
to be cruelty: popular etymology had it that the word *requin* was
derived from *requiem* since a man attacked by sharks would surely

---

[1] *Lautréamont,* p. 9.
[2] *Ibid.,* p. 10.
[3] *Ibid.,* p. 14.

be killed. [4] And certain crabs would rather give up their claws than let go of their prey.

In literature, this type of animal is generally a symbol of evil, for example the sea serpents in the Laocoon episode of the *Aeneid* or the octopus in Hugo's *Les Travailleurs de la mer,* while Christianity has associated many of them with guilty passions. [5] Lautréamont was aware of their consecrated symbolism because he uses them as focus for metaphors with which Maldoror mocks God, in the brothel scene: "Ame royale, livrée dans un moment d'oubli, au crabe de la débauche, au pouple de la faiblesse de caractère, au requin de l'abjection individuelle, au boa de la morale absente, et au colimaçon monstrueux de l'idiotisme!" (p. 247). When these animals are used literally, that is, when they are part of the events, they are described in flattering terms (the shark episode, for instance). Their use, in the above metaphors, based on their traditional pejorative associations, seems therefore ironic: it is as if the speaker adopts, for the purpose of sarcasm, his antagonist's connotations.

The reversal of animal symbolism in *Les Chants* is a logical consequence of the initial reversal, occurring at the beginning of the first stanza, which placed the work, as Pleynet shows, on the side of the taboo, [6] i.e., of the unrepressed life-instinct. These animals are repulsive to us, precisely because civilization requires that we repress our primal aggression, the *vouloir-attaquer*. The animalism in *Les Chants* becomes understandable only if we are able to envisage the release of the instinctive attack: "Ainsi, dès l'instant où l'on pourra créer une poésie de la violence pure, une poésie qui s'enchanterait des libertés de la volonté, on devra lire Lautréamont comme un précurseur." [7]

Bachelard's study concerns itself with the animals that are part of the fiction. There is, however, another aspect to the animalism in *Les Chants* and that is its use in the vehicle of similes. Traditionally, animals have been brought into the fiction by means of the vehicle for expressive or affective purposes. [8] When Baudelaire, in *Spleen*

---

[4] Bloch and von Wartburg, *Dictionnaire étymologique de la langue française* (Paris, 1950).
[5] See, for example, in Jean Daniélou, *Platonisme et théologie mystique* (Paris, 1944), pp. 74-83, the animal symbolism of Grégoire de Nysse.
[6] See above, p. 39 n. 4.
[7] Bachelard, pp. 14-15.
[8] See Stephen Ullmann, *Language and Style,* pp. 147-148: "Yet another limiting factor [in an author's choice of analogies] is *the tone* of the passage and, in a more general way, the author's attitude to his subject. If he wishes to produce a comical or pejorative effect, then certain types of images will be

LXXVIII, compares hope to a bat, he debases the normal associations of the word *L'Espérance* and conveys thereby his feeling of complete depression. [9]

Because the reader becomes aware of the recurrence of animal similes in Lautréamont, they must be treated as a separate category. As in previous chapters, I have thought it best to classify them according to the degree to which they disrupt the reader's habits. The least remarkable comparisons are those which are used in everyday language and are unaffected by the context. The most salient examples are the ones where the reader senses a transposition from a different context, i.e., those in which scientific nomenclature is used. Between these two extremes are the cases in which the animals have a functional purpose, to create a comical or pejorative effect, or to explain the tenor.

1) The comparison is of common usage.

> Alors, pleins de miséricorde, agenouillez-vous ; et que *les hommes, plus nombreux que les poux,* fassent de longues prières.
>
> (I, 7, p. 131)

> O être humain ! te voilà, maintenant, *nu comme un ver,* en présence de mon glaive de diamant !
>
> (II, 1, p. 162)

> Lorsque le berger David atteignit au front le géant Goliath d'une pierre lancée par la fronde, est-ce qu'il n'est pas admirable de remarquer que c'est seulement par la ruse que David a vaincu son adversaire, et que si, au contraire, ils s'étaient pris à bras-le-corps, *le géant l'aurait écrasé comme une mouche.*
>
> (II, 6, p. 175)

In none of the above examples does the comparison appear original enough to attract the reader's attention. Although the first one involves lice, the simile is adjectival rather than verbal. It is the quantity (*nombreux*) which is the link and not some action representing the insect. The animal retains therefore its usual pejorative associations. And, since the comparison precedes the lice stanza (II, 9),

automatically excluded while others will arise almost inevitably. Parallels between human beings and animals will often appear in such contexts since such images are apt to debase man, to reduce him to the level of beasts and to expose the animal side of his nature." See also, Ullmann's commentary on Sartre's insect imagery, pp. 186-188.

[9] *Les Fleurs du mal* (Garnier), pp. 80-81.

it does not contradict any pre-established textual values that would give it greater stylistic significance by providing a contrast with the pattern. Here, as in the other two cases, Lautréamont seems to have drawn on a ready-made image which is likely to go unnoticed.

However, the lack of originality in these similes does not mean that they are unexpressive. They are noticeable *as clichés* which are derogatory. Their presence in the context accomplishes a lowering of the tenor, from human being to lice, worm and fly.

In the following example, this is even more visible because the cliché is renewed:

> Mais toi, ô mon maître, sous ton regard, les habitants des cités sont subitement détruits, comme un tertre de fourmis qu'écrase le talon de l'éléphant.
>
> (IV, 5, p. 270)

The comparison of city-dwellers to ants is commonplace, but the continuation of the analogy rejuvenates the cliché by equating God's look with the heel of an elephant. This unexpected development emphasizes the lowering of both man and God, and calls the reader's attention to the dialectical conflict which, as I shall attempt to show with another image (p. 62), is fundamental in *Les Chants de Maldoror*.

2) The vehicles downgrade the tenor.

These are descriptions of the passengers, in the famous episode where the child runs after a streetcar:

> Sont assis à l'impériale, des hommes qui ont l'œil immobile comme celui d'un poisson mort.
>
> (II, 4, p. 168)

> L'autre baisse la tête d'une manière imperceptible en forme d'acquiescement, et se replonge ensuite dans l'immobilité de son égoïsme, comme une tortue dans sa carapace.
>
> (II, 4, p. 169)

Here, the animals are used as symbols for middle-class insensitivity, since the passengers seem indifferent to the desperation of a child. The *poisson mort* of the first simile acquires significance because, as Bachelard points out, in *Les Chants,* fish and birds are privileged creatures by virtue of the fact that the geometric composition of swimming and of flying gives these animals speed and freedom. [10]

---

[10] Bachelard, p. 50.

The image of a dead fish represents a loss of freedom and corresponds to the lack of motion in the passengers' eyes.

The idea of immobility is repeated in the second example, which appears a few lines further down, in reference to another man on the streetcar. In this case, the vehicle explains the metaphoric *se replonge,* since that would create a milieu in which free motion is possible. While *tortue* connotes slowness, *carapace* has associations of both a protective shield (selfishness) and an enclosure (restriction of freedom, imprisonment). Moreover, the nominal structure in the tenor—*l'immobilité de son égoïsme*—reinforces the impression of stagnation by making an abstract concept out of a lack of motion. This produces a structural parallelism with the concrete noun *sa carapace,* and the image becomes more vivid because the analogy is clearer than if it were, for instance, with *son égoïsme immobile.*

The following example is from the stanza in which Maldoror has followed Mervyn home in order to find out his address. He is planning to seduce him and then to murder him:

> Il [Maldoror] s'avance, comme une hyène, sans être vu, et longe les côtés de la cour.
>
> (VI, II, p. 333)

The hyena is traditionally a symbol for treachery and underhanded cruelty. In reference to human beings, the animal has connotations of deviousness and of villainy. [11] The comparison in this case helps to underline the sinister atmosphere, suggested by *sans être vu* and by *longe,* and is ominous of the perfidious deed Maldoror intends to commit.

The downgrading is much stronger when the vehicle subject matter is repulsive. In the eighth stanza of Chant II, the narrator tells his story: being tired of this world, he has looked up at the mysteries of heaven and has dared to penetrate them. There, he saw God, seated on a throne made of gold and of human excrement, eating the rotten trunk of a man.

> Ses pieds plongeaient dans une vaste mare de sang en ébullition, *à la surface duquel s'élevaient* tout à coup, *comme des ténias à travers le contenu d'un pot de chambre, deux ou trois têtes imprudentes,* qui s'abaissaient aussitôt, avec la rapidité de la flèche : un coup de pied bien appliqué sur l'os du nez était

---

11 Cf. Chateaubriand, *Mémoires d'outre-tombe,* II, I, 7: "Fouché... avait l'air d'une hyène habillée; il haleinait les futures effluves du sang."

> la récompense connue de la révolte au règlement, occasionnée
> par le besoin de respirer un autre milieu ; car, enfin, ces hom-
> mes n'étaient pas des poissons !
>
> (II, 8, p. 182)

Excrement and filth are generally considered attributes of the
Devil. [12] By describing God in terms of Satan and heaven as hell,
Lautréamont fuses the two in the reader's mind. We can no longer
be sure of what was meant by *le Créateur,* and we find that what
we expected to be below is really above: *les mystères du ciel.*

The vehicle of the simile is in a disjunction between the verb and
the inverted subject of the tenor. A more direct syntactic structure
would be *à la surface du sang en ébullition, deux ou trois têtes
imprudentes s'élevaient, comme des ténias à travers le contenu d'un
pot de chambre.* By placing the vehicle between the two parts of the
tenor, attention is called to it.

The comparison of human heads to ringworms is derogatory and
repulsive, but the lack of precision in *deux ou trois* and the detached-
sounding adjective *imprudentes* make the comparison seem casual.
In the vehicle, *le contenu d'un pot de chambre* appears as a feigned
delicacy, a pseudo-euphemism, [13] and creates therefore an ironic effect.

In the part of the sentence which follows the simile, the exaggerated speed of *qui s'abaissaient aussitôt, avec la rapidité de la
flèche* gives the impression that the narrator is dismissing the matter
too easily. This is reinforced by the explanation of the event, after

---

[12] See Norman O. Brown, *Life against Death,* pp. 206-207: "Psychoanalytic
studies of the Devil, following Freud himself, have emphasized the Oedipal
aspect of the Devil, his status as a father-substitute, the ambivalent combination of emulation of and hostility against the father in the Devil (as
father-substitutes) underlying their opposition. The persistently anal character
of the Devil has not been emphasized enough. The color preeminently
associated with the Devil and the Black Mass is black — not because
of his place of abode (a circular explanation) but because of the association
of black and filth. 'The painters paint the Devil black and filthy' says Luther.
Equally persistent is the association of the Devil with a sulphurous or other
evil smell, the origin of which is plainly revealed in the article '*De crepitu
Diaboli*' in an eighteenth century compendium of folklore. The climax of the
ritual of the witches' Sabbath was to kiss the Devil's posteriors. In the central
ceremony of the Black Mass, as the Queen of Sabbath lay prone, 'The sacred
host was prepared by kneading on her buttocks a mixture of the most repulsive
material, faeces, menstrual blood, urine, and offal of various kinds.' Hence
Dante makes the still point of the turning world, round which he passes
upward to Purgatory, Satan's anus; hence Bosch, in the panel depicting this
world as Hell, enthrones Satan on a privy, from which the souls that have
passed out of his anus drop into the black pit."

[13] See Stephen Ullmann, *Semantics: an Introduction to the Science of
Meaning* (New York, 1962), p. 207.

a colon. The clarification of the action brings in a linguistic level (French school colloquialisms such as *un coup de pied bien appliqué,* the ironic *la récompense,* and *la révolte au règlement*) which is totally unexpected in a description of heaven. It may be that, for psychological reasons, the lycée experience is, in Lautréamont's eyes, the equivalent of hell and that all authorities (God, the school master, etc.) become one devil. [14] To the reader, however, the description of an inferno in terms associated with school is likely to appear as a frivolous treatment of a serious subject, i.e., as black humor. And the abstract judgment of the situation (*car enfin ces hommes n'étaient pas des poissons !*) seems, in context, to be mock-sympathy. The sentence with the animal simile as center fuses the subjective (repulsive) with the objective (irony) and denies the reader's expectation of clearly defined categories.

3) The vehicle illustrates an action in the tenor.

The second stanza of Chant IV, one of the key passages in the book, [15] begins with a series of assertions and denials: "Deux piliers, qu'il n'était pas difficile et encore moins possible de prendre pour des baobabs, s'apercevaient dans la vallée, plus grands que deux épingles. En effet, c'étaient deux tours énormes. Et quoique deux baobabs, au premier coup d'œil, ne ressemblent pas à deux épingles, ni même à deux tours, cependant, en employant habilement les ficelles de la prudence, on peut affirmer, sans crainte d'avoir tort..." (p. 252). This is followed by a long, even more nonsensical, digression. Marcelin Pleynet comments that these contradictions serve to emphasize the arbitrariness of all fiction: "... la fiction, prise dans la logique purement conventionnelle du récit (le lecteur doit ajouter foi à l'invraisemblable ou abandonner sa lecture), se trouve en proie à l'envahissement de toutes les fictions possibles, celle que l'auteur choisit n'étant finalement ni plus ni moins arbitraire qu'aucune autre." [16] But he dismisses too easily the explanation which Lautréamont provides two pages further down: "... quand au commencement j'ai comparé les

---

[14] See Bachelard, "La violence humaine et les complexes de la culture," in *Lautréamont,* pp. 60-73. Bachelard points out that the psychological motivation of Lautréamont's aggressiveness probably has its source in the repression imposed on the adolescent during the school years. (Cf. the "Quand un élève interne..." passage, p. 152).

[15] André Breton considered the passage significant enough to include in his *Anthologie de l'humour noir* (Paris, 1950), pp. 102-106.

[16] Pleynet, p. 68.

piliers aux épingles avec tant de justesse... je me suis basé sur les lois de l'optique qui ont établi que, plus le rayon visuel est éloigné d'un objet, plus l'image se reflète à diminution de la rétine." (p. 254) For Pleynet, this is simply another conventional justification borrowed from the *roman noir* genre. [17] But it is more than that. It has the factual appearance of a physics manual formula.   Coming, as it does, immediately after a pattern of nonsensical contradictions, it presents a striking contrast which cannot but catch the reader's attention.   As an inescapable element it forces the reader to wonder about its significance.   Consequently, the information in the statement acquires a more generalized meaning: the subject decides what the object is.   Not only does the optical law, to which Lautréamont appeals here, tell the reader that the object (the fiction) is arbitrary, but it also repeats what Pleynet had pointed out about the first stanza, namely that the subject of *Les Chants* had no object except itself. When, in the first few lines of the book, the author said that the reader should become like the pages he is about to read, the fundamental dialectical problem (the division of subject and object, the separation of the reader from the text) was stated.   For what remains constant, in the passage under discussion, in spite of all the contradictions, is the duality: *deux piliers, deux épingles, deux tours* and the subject and the object (the author and the fiction).   The problem is to overcome the dialectical situation, to become reunified.

This is made explicit further in the stanza. Having said that he will be appreciated because he was not hypocritical enough to disregard the evil side of human nature, Lautréamont uses the following simile to illustrate his struggle:

> Dans ses combats surnaturels, il [Lautréamont, Maldoror] attaquera l'homme et le Créateur, comme quand l'espadon enfonce son épée dans le ventre de la baleine...
>
> (IV, 2, p. 257)

On the page where this image occurs, there is an abrupt shift from first person to third person, fusing Lautréamont and Maldoror. The reader can, therefore, not differenciate between author and character, between the text and reality.   In the tenor of the simile, the pronoun *il* represents the dissolution of the duality of the protagonist, but the enemy remains double (*l'homme et le créateur*).   In

---

[17] *Ibid.,* pp. 71-72.

the vehicle, however, they too become fused into one animal: *la baleine*. All that remains are the two antagonistic forces—the Slave and the Master, David and Goliath. And even this last duality is about to be resolved since *enfoncer son épée dans le ventre* implies, in this context, attacking by penetrating, by becoming part of. Moreover, *la baleine* is a fusion of God and the Devil, since the whale, in medieval bestiaries, often symbolized the Devil. [18] The vehicle illustrates the moral and historical conflict by transposing it on a zoological level.

In a similar way, Lautréamont uses animal vehicles to explain his method of composition, the psychological problem involved in reading *Les Chants* and the effect which it produces on the reader.

When, in the first stanza of Chant I, Lautréamont warned the reader to be careful before going any further into the book, he suggested that the reader follow the example of the cranes. The cranes fly in triangular formation towards a determined point on the horizon. The first crane, who is the oldest, sensing an oncoming storm, changes the direction of the triangle and "parce qu'elle n'est pas bête, elle prend ainsi un autre chemin philosophique et plus sûr" (p. 124). But the reader who, unlike the crane, persists in continuing the book and reaches the first stanza of Chant V, will be told why the book is so difficult: "Que le lecteur ne se fâche pas contre moi, si ma prose n'a pas le bonheur de lui plaire. Tu soutiens que mes idées sont au moins singulières. Ce que tu dis là, homme respectable, est la vérité ; mais une vérité partiale. Or, quelle source abondante d'erreurs et de méprises n'est pas toute vérité partiale" (p. 285). This is followed by the description of the flight of the starlings. [19] The birds fly forward in the manner of a whirlwind, each individual bird flying towards the center and then away from it, so that all the circles lead to one central point. In spite of this strange manner of proceeding,

---

[18] See Francis Carmody, "Le Diable des bestiaires," *CAIEF*, July 1953, p. 82 : "La baleine est aussi choisie comme symbole du Diable [in the *Physiologus*]. Les malheureux matelots qui, la prenant pour une île, débarquent sur son dos, sont imprudents plutôt que coupables..."
[19] Maurice Viroux, "Lautréamont et le Dr. Chenu," *Mercure de France*, 1070, December 1952, p. 639, established that this flight was copied from Buffon, probably through the encyclopedia of Dr. Chenu.
From the point of view of affectivity, the precise source of any passage is irrelevant. What is important is its situation in context and its effect upon the reader. For the stylistician, the fact that certain passages prompt researchers to find sources is indicative of their effect.
See also Maurice Saillet, "Défense du plagiat," *Les Lettres nouvelles*, April 1953, pp. 205-214.

the band as a whole moves ahead very rapidly. "Toi, de même, ne fais pas attention à la manière bizarre dont je chante chacune de ces strophes. Mais sois persuadé que les accents fondamentaux de la poésie n'en conservent pas moins leur intrinsèque droit sur mon intelligence" (p. 286). Lautréamont thus indicates precisely the reaction of the reader whose perception of reality and mode of thinking is linear (the cranes fly in a straight line) when he encounters a text whose development is circular.

Paul Zweig has pointed out that the circularity of *Les Chants* is a narcissistic manifestation: "Le poète fait tourbillonner autour de lui la foule de ses images, découpant un espace personnel dans celui, 'infini', de la réalité. Son tourbillon crée un monde dont le seul centre est le poète lui-même. Il s'agit d'un geste proprement narcissique. Enfermé dans le cercle de ses images Lautréamont est littéralement au centre du monde." [20] The poet therefore incorporates into the text, into the creation of his own personality (since Lautréamont is non-existent, an assumed name taken from a fictional character), the world around him: plagiarisms, literary precedents, his own judgments on what he has just written, the reader, etc. [21] The text is inclusive and must of necessity be discontinuous. A continuous, logical composition would have to be exclusive, selecting and creating limitations. [22] Because the development is discontinuous, it must constantly begin anew, hence the stanzas become separate entities which seem to have no relationship to one another. Yet, like the starlings, they move forward as a group: from Chant I which is the most orthodox and which Lautréamont considered only a trial, [23] to the clear understanding of what he was trying to do, in Chant V, to the fragmentations of Chant VI, to the aphoristic form of *Poésies*.

---

[20] Paul Zweig, "Lautréamont ou les violences du Narcisse," *ALM*, 74, 1967 (1), p. 11.

[21] Lucienne Rochon, "Le Professeur de rhétorique de Lauréamont: Gustave Hinstin," *Europe*, 449, September 1966, pp. 153-189. She suggests, on p. 184, that Lautréamont's comments on what he has just written (statements like *comparaison trop commune, excuse passable, comparaison qui manque de vérité*) could very well be annotations which his teacher had made on his homework and which he incorporated into his own text.

[22] Cf. *Unpublished Letters of Samuel Taylor Coleridge* (Yale University Press, 1933), II, 128: "The common end of all *narrative,* nay, of *all,* Poems is to convert a *series* into a *Whole:* to make those events, which in real or imagined History move on in a *straight* line, assume to our Understandings a *circular* motion — the snake with its tail in its mouth."

[23] "Ne soyez pas sévère pour celui qui ne fait encore qu'essayer sa lyre: elle rend un son si étrange!... La fin du dix-neuvième siècle verra son poète (cependant, au début, il ne doit pas commencer par un chef-d'œuvre, mais suivre la loi de la nature)", p. 160.

4) the vehicle of the simile is scientific.

In the third stanza of Chant IV, Maldoror is hiding from the two madwomen who have come to check on the young man they had hung from the gallows by his hair, because he refused to submit to his mother's sexual advances:

> Je me recachai derrière le buisson, et je me tins coi, comme l'acantophorus serraticornis, qui ne montre que la tête en dehors de son nid.
>
> (VI, 3, p. 259)

Here, the vehicle suddenly breaks the dramatic intensity of the situation because the technical vocabulary (*acantophorus serraticornis*) renders the comparison incomprehensible and comical, the name of the bird sounding ridiculous. This is due to the Latin form whose sequence of syllables is phonetically grotesque for French ears. They are the type of words which schoolchildren create when they want to mimic Latin nouns, and which are used in literature to satirize pedantry (Rabelais, Diafoirus, father and son in *Le Malade imaginaire,* etc.). Yet, the adjectival clause *qui ne montre que la tête en dehors de son nid,* explaining the analogy, clarifies the words by indicating that they refer to an actual bird, that they are not made up. The comparison is both ridiculous and precise. But the clarification also reveals the humor of the situation: the picture of Maldoror looking out from behind a bush like a bird with its head protruding from a nest. The power of the taboo theme is dissolved by the scientific terminology, whose comical overtones may give the impression of black humor. This, in turn, is weakened by the factual explanation which, through its juxtaposition to the tenor renews the humorous effect. The reader's expectations are deceived as soon as they are created because all the distinctions of genres and of language levels are erased, and all points of reference disappear.

Lautréamont, watching his reader's reaction to the text, assumes that if the latter has reached the beginning of Chant V without abandoning the book, he must be willing to continue: "N'est-il pas vrai, mon ami, que jusqu'à un certain point, ta sympathie est acquise à mes chants? Or, qui t'empêche de franchir les autres degrés? La frontière entre ton goût et le mien est invisible; tu ne pourras jamais la saisir: preuve que cette frontière elle-même n'existe pas." (pp. 286-287). The author is fully aware that the difficulty which the reader experiences is due to taste, to cultural conditioning: "Il n'est pas utile pour toi que tu t'encroûtes dans la cartilagineuse carapace d'un axiome que tu crois inébranlable. Il y a d'autres axiomes aussi qui sont inébranlables, et qui marchent parallèlement avec le tien." (p. 287). For the reader who brings to the text a linear perception of reality (Cartesian logic, classical aesthetic standards, repressive moral values, etc.), the involvement in a circular perception (narcissistic, inclusive, lack of categorization and of repressions, etc.) can be a painful sensation. [24] It is, however, not fatal:

> Et, de même que les rotifères et les tardigrades peuvent être chauffés à une température voisine de l'ébullition, sans perdre nécessairement leur vitalité, il en sera de même pour toi, si tu sais t'assimiler, avec précaution, l'âcre sérosité suppurative qui se dégage avec lenteur de l'agacement que causent mes intéressantes élucubrations.
>
> (V, 1, p. 287)

Since the scientific vehicle precedes the tenor, it has a mystifying effect, which is abruptly clarified by the tenor. [25] The reader then realizes that what he was about to dismiss as nonsense (because the precision of the signifiers seemed to have no referent) is, after all, an accurate analogy: *le rotifères et les tardigrades* corresponds to *toi*, the reader, *peuvent être chauffés* to *si tu sait t'assimiler*, *à une température voisine* to *avec précaution* and *l'ébullition* to *l'âcre sérosité suppurative qui se dégage avec lenteur de mes intéressantes élucu-*

---

[24] We can see what Lautréamont meant, by the reaction of someone like Suzanne Bernard, whose initial defense is to classify Lautréamont's more disruptive images as arbitrary: "Il semble que du début à la fin de l'œuvre, cet emploi de la métaphore soit devenu de plus en plus conscient et voulu; et qu'en même temps le rapprochement forcé 'des objets les plus opposés entre eux' ait fini par tourner au système, par devenir absolument gratuit et artificiel: un procédé d'humour tout mécanique, s'apparentant à ceux dont Lautréamont use, je l'ai dit, pour exercer contre la technique littéraire sa verve destructrice", *Le Poème en prose*, p. 244. But, on the next page, she admits that this type of image produces a liberation: "Cette soudaineté du rapprochement, cette brusque liaison imposée de force à notre esprit, qui nous déconcerte d'abord, puis nous paraît un élément de beauté et de poésie par le sentiment de découverte qu'il suscite en nous, par la nouveauté féconde de la vision, par l'étrangeté même (qui ne se dissipe pas toujours à la réflexion) de la démarche analogique."

[25] Marguerite Bonnet, "Lautréamont et Michelet," *RHLF*, December 1964, p. 617, has found that Lautréamont probably borrowed this detail about the rotifera and the tardigrada's boiling point from the writings of Dr. Pouchet, one of Michelet's scientific sources. Pouchet was an opponent of Pasteur on the question of spontaneous generation, and had conducted numerous experiments attempting to prove that these organisms could not resist temperatures above 100 degrees. They could therefore safely "être chauffés à une température voisine de l'ébullition."

brations. The point of contact, the link, is *sans perdre nécessaire-ment leur vitalité.* The reader's relationship to the text is compared to a laboratory experiment. The scientific vehicle is an illustration of what we experience when we read Lautréamont. Yet, like the organisms which do not necessarily lose their life in nearboiling water, the reader does not lose any vitality through his contact with the text. The tenor explains what is necessary in order to survive: we must absorb the repulsive emanations (*l'âcre sérosité suppurative*) of the writing or, rather, of the annoyance which results from the strange way of writing. The last part of the tenor, *l'agacement que causent mes intéressantes élucubrations,* is the author's commentary, indicating that he is aware of the psychological effect produced (l'agacement), and viewing himself ironically (mes intéressantes élucubrations). In this way, the image shifts from scientific reality to the reality of the reader and then to that of the poet, while the text itself is viewed as mere literature, because of the self-denigrating comment upon it.

The transposition of scientific material into a literary context affects the vehicle, the tenor, and the simile as a whole. In the context of the stanza, the sudden appearance of a scientific formula makes it seem isolated, an effect without a cause. The very precision of the language is mystifying to anyone who is not a specialist. The reader is therefore aware of the connotations of *les rotifères et les tardigrades* rather than of their denotation. And on the connotative level these words may seem comical, suggesting vulgarity (from *roter*) and slowness (from *tarder*). Since they correspond to *the reader,* in the tenor, this creates not only a lowering from man to microscopic animal, but also a mocking tone. Moreover, while the analogy between the two terms of the comparison is exact, the reader may find that it is exaggerated. The annoyance which can be felt when one reads *Les Chants* is not as painful as the experiment described in the vehicle. Neither is the effect, even when unpleasant, anything as repulsive as *l'âcre sérosité suppurative.* The biological references of the simile become hyperbolic in context, and this transforms the plagiarized material into an ironic device: it is as if the author were telling the reader to take neither the work nor himself too seriously. Hence, the impression of reason, which the scientific precision gives the analogy, is deceptive. It blurs, rather than clarifies, our vision.

Similarly, the following simile has a scientific vehicle which precedes the tenor. The narrator has been watching a beetle who was

pushing a ball, made of excrement, to the foot of a hill. He cautiously
follows the insect.

> Le scarabée était arrivé au bas du tertre. J'avais emboîté mon
> pas sur ses traces, et j'étais encore à une grande distance du
> lieu de la scène ; car, de même que les stercoraires, oiseaux
> inquiets comme s'ils étaient toujours affamés, se plaisent dans
> les mers qui baignent les deux pôles, et n'avancent qu'acciden-
> tellement dans les zones tempérées, ainsi je n'étais pas tran-
> quille, et je portais mes jambes en avant avec beaucoup de
> lenteur.
>
> (V, 2, p. 290)

As in the rotifera image, the reader faces a long, seemingly
unrelated, detailed description, before he can realize that it is an
illustration of the action in the tenor. [26] Then, he sees that it is an
analogy of motion, and not one of form. This prompts rereading to
find the verb which is hidden in the specialized context of the vehicle.
Once it has been discovered that *avancent* corresponds to *je portais
mes jambes en avant,* the other points of the comparison become
clear: *oiseaux inquiets* corresponds to *je n'étais pas tranquille, accidentellement dans les zones tempérées* to *en avant avec beaucoup de
lenteur.* From the encyclopedia accounts, Lautréamont selects the
elements which are non-scientific and anthropomorphic (*inquiets
comme s'ils étaient toujours affamés, se plaisent dans les mers,
n'avancent qu'accidentellement*), and it is on these that he builds his
analogies. The subjective words in the scientific statements are
brought to the fore and make the comparison possible.

Furthermore, unlike a traditional simile, in which the vehicle may
be used to explain the tenor, the above examples reverse the process,
since the vehicle is incomprehensible until it is explained by the tenor.
In a conventional development, the poet uses his imagination to provide, by means of the vehicle, an analogy which would make the
tenor (the fiction) more vivid or more believable. By reversing this
method and by bringing scientific facts into the fiction, Lautréamont
makes it appear that the tenor is arbitrarily chosen to justify the
vehicle. The reader is thus reminded that it is the fiction which is
imaginary and the *brought in* element which is real. In a poetic
context, however, this outside reality acquires subjective connotations

---

[26] This description is also plagiarized from Dr. Chenu's encyclopedia. See
Maurice Viroux, *loc. cit.,* p. 638.

which make it seem fictional. It is not, therefore, a simple interchange of imagination and reality but a fusion of the two.

These similes, in which a scientific vehicle precedes the tenor, produce three consequences. First, the reader's normal reading speed is broken by the mystification. He is forced to participate by exerting himself to understand. There is, as a result, an application of the slow motion which is referred to in both tenors (*l'âcre sérosité suppurative qui se dégage avec lenteur..., et je portais mes jambes en avant avec beaucoup de lenteur.*). Secondly, because of the involvement created by the mystification, the disruptive effect of these images will remain in the reader's memory. And thirdly, after close examination, he finds that Lautréamont is revealing to him a new mode of perception, a vision which is not restricted by the artificial limits imposed through culture, since the boundaries between the objective and the subjective have vanished. In this respect, the surrealists' debt to Lautréamont is clearly acknowledged: "C'est entre 1866 et 1875 que les poètes entreprirent de réunir systématiquement ce qui semblait à tout jamais séparé. Lautréamont le fit plus délibérément qu'aucun autre." [27]

---

[27] Paul Eluard, *Donner à voir* (Gallimard, 1939), p. 129.

CHAPTER V

SIMILES COMBINED WITH METAPHORS

The simile-metaphor combinations in *Les Chants de Maldoror* can be divided into three categories, which I have again classified according to the degree of intensity of their effect: 1) the vehicle of the simile, although it may have its own relatively remarkable metaphor, explains or modifies a metaphoric tenor, 2) the vehicle of the simile contains a striking metaphor which overshadows the tenor, and 3) the vehicle of the simile is part of a general metaphoric development, so that the metaphor, rather than the simile, catches the reader's attention. This does not mean that the effect of the simile is cancelled by the metaphor, but that the metaphor is the characteristic which strikes first. It is a question of hierarchy of effects rather than of incompatibility.

1) the vehicle explains or modifies a metaphoric tenor.

In Chant V, God appears to the narrator in the form of a snake. After the initial bafflement, He is recognized:

> Et qui est-tu, toi-même, substance audacieuse ? Non !... Non !... je ne me trompe pas ; et malgré les métamorphoses multiples auxquelles tu as recours, toujours ta tête de serpent reluira devant mes yeux, comme un phare d'éternelle injustice, et de cruelle domination.
>
> (V, 4, p. 300)

At this point, the reader does not yet actually know that the apparition is God, although he suspects it. He cannot be sure until the next page, when the speaker addresses Him as *ta Providence*.

In the tenor, *tête de serpent* is literal since this is the way God is showing Himself. The focus of the metaphorical statement [1], *reluira*,

---

[1] The *metaphorical statement* is, in Black's terminology, the double unit of *focus* and *frame*.

is explained by *phare,* the focus of the vehicle, whose frame consists of two abstract nouns, *injustice* and *domination,* each modified by a preceding, abstract adjective, *éternelle* and *cruelle. Phare,* used figuratively, connotes *that which serves as a guide, which gives light* and is therefore ameliorative. The first attribute, *éternelle injustice* is in context, ironic since the adjective, suggesting *l'Eternel* and reinforcing the impression of permanence given by *toujours,* leads us to expect *justice* rather than *injustice.* The second attribute, *cruelle domination,* brings to mind the God of the Old Testament [2] and, by the anteposition of the adjective, suggests that the domination is primarily moral. Thus, God, having been transformed into a serpent, the animal associated with the Devil, takes on physically and morally repulsive attributes. The image reveals the nature of the snake, while the God/Devil reversal contradicts established connotations and expresses the narrator's antagonistic attitude.

In the seventh stanza of Chant I, Maldoror describes the method of torturing a child and the pleasurable taste of blood and tears, gathered in one's hand:

---

[2] Maldoror's struggle with God strongly suggests Biblical parallels. The hero, at times, seems to be the fallen angel: "mais, celui que n'a pas pu oublier le Créateur, depuis le jour glorieux où, renversant de leur socle les annales du ciel, où, par je ne sais quel tripotage infâme, étaient consignées *sa* puissance et *son* éternité, j'appliquai mes quatre cents ventouses sur le dessous de son aiselle, et lui fit pousser des cris terribles..." (p. 215.) "Il y a longtemps de ça; mais, je crois que maintenant il sait où est ma demeure; il se garde d'y rentrer; nous vivons, tous les deux, comme deux monarques voisins qui connaissent leurs forces respectives, ne peuvent se vaincre l'un l'autre, et sont fatigués des batailles inutiles du passé." (p. 216.) It is probable that *Paradise Lost* was among Lautréamont's sources. In a letter to the publisher Verbroekhoven, he had written: "J'ai chanté le mal comme on fait Mickiewickz, Byron, Milton, Southey, A. de Musset, Baudelaire, etc." (p. 398.) But if the reader thinks that he has established that Maldoror represents the Devil, his expectations will again be deceived, for in Chant VI, the protagonist is described as more powerful than Satan: "A son nom (Maldoror's), les armées célestes tremblent; et plus d'un raconte, dans les régions que j'ai quittées, que Satan lui-même, Satan, l'incarnation du mal, n'est pas si redoutable." p. 346-347.)

One commentator, H. R. Linder, *Lautréamont: sein Werk und sein Weltbild* (Bâle, 1947), defends the thesis that the main source of *Les Chants* is the *Apocalypse.* But, as Blanchot concludes, after discussing Linder's theory and pointing out several similarities between *Les Chants* and *Les Fleurs du Mal,* "Il est frappant que Lautréamont, même s'il suit le courant de son siècle, même lorsqu'il exprime avec l'insolence de la jeunesse les partis pris et les passions de circonstance, exaltation du mal, goût du macabre, défi luciférien, sans doute ne trompe pas ces sources, mais, en même temps, semble hanté par toutes les grandes œuvres de tous les siècles et finalement apparaisse errant dans un monde de fiction où, formés par tous et destinés à tous, se rejoignent et se confirment les rêves vagues des religions et des mythologies sans mémoire. " *Lautréamont et Sade,* p. 261.

> ... *laquelle main* ensuite se dirigeait fatalement vers la bouche,
> qui puisait à longs traits, dans *cette coupe, tremblante comme*
> *les dents de l'élève qui regarde obliquement celui qui est né*
> *pour l'oppresser,* les larmes ?
>
> (I, 7, p. 128)

The tenor is itself close to a stated simile since both terms (*la main, cette coupe*) are expressed, but the connecting process, i.e. the substitution of a figurative word for a previously stated literal word, with a demonstrative adjective as *pointing device,* is more immediate than the usual linking words of explicit comparisons. The vehicle is situated in a place of emphasis between the verb *puisait* and its object *les larmes.* This creates a disruptive effect by leaving the reader suspended over a rather long disjunction. The adjective *tremblante* in apposition to the focus of the tenor provides the link to the vehicle, which introduces the theme of the oppressed schoolboy, anticipating the famous passage about lycée life. Now, *tremblante* seems at first to be merely descriptive of *coupe* and to refer to the nervous pleasure of drinking tears. However, by introducing this particular vehicle, by acting as the word which makes the comparison plausible, the connotation of *tremblante* changes from pleasure to fear. The note of sympathy brought in by the vehicle is all the more surprising to the reader because it comes after a lengthy sadistic advice on how to torture infants. The vehicle is emphasized by both the position in the sentence and by its unexpected theme. The reason for this emphasis seems quite clear: it provides the philosophical justification for the cruelty which is being advocated, since sadism is a result of what Bachelard calls Lautréamont's cultural complex. [3] This theme is then elaborated in stanza twelve of the same Chant:

> ... il [un élève interne] sent les flots tumultueux d'une haine
> vivace, monter comme une épaisse fumée, à son cerveau, qui lui
> paraît près d'éclater.
>
> (I, 12, p. 152)

The fear, suggested by *tremblante,* has turned into hatred. *Haine* is the frame and primary subject of the metaphor in the tenor. The literal *larmes* of the previous image have become the figurative *flots tumultueux* which rise inside the oppressed mind, till it is ready to explode. The other modifier of *haine, vivace,* has not only its normal

---

[3] Bachelard, *Lautréamont,* pp. 60-76.

figurative meaning (deep-rooted, vigorous) but also its more strict botanical meaning (a long-living plant). Hence, in the tenor, we have another example of Lautréamont's fusing of elements. The vehicle, moreover, introduces a third element (fire), by implication. Thus hatred becomes visualized as liquid and shapeless (*les flots tumul-tueux*), deep-rooted with a plant-like capacity for growth, untouchable yet befogging (*épaisse fumée*), and when this phenomenon reaches the mind, the schoolboy is likely to become insane. In this example, then, the vehicle serves to modify the tenor and to reinforce and complete the metaphoric description of a feeling.

2) the vehicle of the simile contains a metaphor.

Mervyn, whom Maldoror is trying to seduce in order to kill him, is writing a letter, to the handsome stranger, in which he expresses reservations:

> Comment dire cela ? Quand je pense à vous, *ma poitrine s'agite, retentissante comme l'écroulement d'un empire en décadence...*
>
> (VI, iii, p. 338)

The vehicle explains the hyperbolic *retentissante*. The transformation of the verbal cliché *un empire qui s'écroule* into a nominal form creates a difficulty of perception for the reader, thus calling attention to itself, because it blurs the analogy. We would expect *ma poitrine s'agite, retentissante comme un empire qui s'écroule,* i.e. a concrete subject and verb in the vehicle corresponding to a concrete subject and verb in the tenor. By substituting an abstract noun for a concrete verb and by maintaining the content of the cliché and linking it to the concrete tenor of the simile, Lautréamont succeeds in emphasizing the change in perspective created by the juxtaposition of a crumbling empire and an excited chest. [4] This subverts the general tone of the letter and leaves us, once more, confused because it makes us doubt the sincerity of the emotion expressed. The disproportion is so great that the effect is ironic.

In stanza three of Chant V, Lautréamont vows that he will never sleep:

> Tant qu'un reste de sève brûlante coulera dans mes os, comme un torrent de métal fondu, je ne dormirai point.
>
> (V, 3, p. 295)

---

[4] For the various uses of the abstract for the concrete see Riffaterre, *Le Style des Pléiades*, pp. 164-171.

Here, both the tenor and the vehicle contain a metaphor, although the reader cannot be quite sure that *sève* is used metaphorically for *sang* or *moelle* since the narrator's humanity is not established. But a metaphor by *replacement* is likely to be the first impression that *sève* produces, since the word is often used metaphorically for moral energy or vigor and, the theme being will power, *brûlante* acquires the figurative meaning of *intense*. The verb *coulera* implies liquid motion so that the impression that *sève* stands for blood is established. Yet, the adverb of place *dans mes os* suggests marrow rather than blood. Since we are not dealing with a mimetic representation of the world, we must disregard the concept of *mixed* metaphors and accept the possibility of anatomical change or fusion. Nonetheless, *dans mes os* is likely to create a discordant note in the reader's mind. But the vehicle returns us to the initial assumption: *torrent* also suggests liquid, intense motion, validating the plausibility of the link *coulera*. And *métal fondu* completes the analogy since it also connotes thickness, fluidity and heat. Thus, while the comparison works out on the figurative level because of the logic of the parallelism, it remains unsettling on the literal level where it does not develop logically (from the botanical *sève* to the animal *dans mes os* to the mineral *métal*), making interpretation impossible. By a series of self-controverting attributes, in Beardsley's terminology, the comparison performs a change in reality yet leaves the moral correspondance between the various elements, used metaphorically, intact. A disruptive effect occurs because the figurative similarity contradicts the literal possibility of the image. [5]

3) the simile is part of the general metaphoric development.

Maldoror has just spoken of his background and is now explaining his rebellion against God and humanity. He is about to discover God's cruelty:

> Un jour donc, *fatigué de talonner du pied le sentier abrupt du voyage terrestre, et de m'en aller, en chancelant comme un homme ivre, à travers les catacombes obscures de la vie,* je

---

[5] Cf. Baudelaire, "Les Sept Vieillards": "Les mystères partout coulent comme des sèves / Dans les canaux étroits du colosse puissant." *Les Fleurs du Mal* (Garnier), p. 97. About this poem, Baudelaire wrote to Jean Morel: "C'est le premier numéro d'une nouvelle série que je veux tenter, et je crains bien d'avoir simplement réussi à dépasser les limites assignées à la poésie." *Correspondance générale* (Conard) II, p. 324.

> soulevai avec lenteur mes yeux spleenétiques, cernés d'un grand
> cercle bleuâtre, vers la concavité du firmament, et j'osai péné-
> trer, moi, si jeune, les mystères du ciel !
>
> (II, 8, p. 182)

The image resembles the beginning of Chant I, where Lautréamont warns the reader against carelessly entering the unexplored
territory of the poem. The vocabulary of the frame is almost identical
to that of the first stanza: *dirige tes talons en arrière, son chemin
abrupt et sauvage.* And while Maldoror, in the above, dares to
pénétrer... les mystères du ciel, the reader had been told to be careful
before *pénétrer de pareilles landes inexplorées,* i.e. the book. The
common meaning of *talonner* is *to pursue closely and energetically,*
but its immediate context seems to suggest the rarer meaning *to hit
with the heel, to walk.* [6] The simile *en chancelant comme un homme
ivre,* not particularly striking as such, clarifies the ambiguity by
verifying the second impression. But, although the vocabulary and
the theme are almost the same, they were figurative in the opening
and are now literal. *Dirige tes talons en arrière* was used metaphorically, since it was an indication to the reader to stop reading, while
fatigué de talonner du pied le sentier abrupt du voyage terrestre
refers quite literally to Maldoror's travels and the weariness they produced. Yet it has the appearance of being figurative, first because of
the reminiscence of its initial context, secondly because *sentier* is in
the singular, making it less concrete than *les sentiers* and, thirdly,
because *voyage terrestre* can easily be viewed as a metaphor for *la
vie.* The same lack of a clear distinction applies to *catacombes
obscures* which can be literal, as an adverb of *m'en aller... à travers,*
or figurative with *la vie.* If we read the statement literally, as the
context leads us to do, space and time (*voyage terrestre* and *la vie*)
become fused and logic disrupted. If, in our desire to understand,
we read the statement figuratively, and maintain the symbolic analogy
between *sentier abrupt/catacombes obscures* and *voyage terrestre/
la vie,* we violate the context and the story itself becomes confusing.
The image is striking because it blurs the line of separation between
the figurative and the literal, between reality and imagination.

This fusion is also significant when one tries to explain the similarity between the above quotation and the beginning of Chant I: the

---

[6] Cf. Roland Dorgelès, *Les Croix de Bois* (A. Michel, 1919), p. 236: "En
avant!... Marche!... Le départ avait été pesant mais déjà la cadence se faisait
plus nette, et les pieds talonnaient la route d'un rythme régulier."

literal *lecteur* is about to enter the figurative *landes inexplorées,* a work of imagination, while the imaginary hero of the book enters the real *mystères du ciel.* The expected analogy is that Maldoror enters the unknown territory as the reader would contemplate the mysteries of heaven. The interchange makes Maldoror as real as the reader and the reader no more important than a fictitious character; the poem becomes reality, and reality a product of the literary imagination.

In the following example, the remarkable feature is not the difficulty of separating the figurative from the literal, but the apparent lack of a structural indication which would avoid the possibility of confusion. The narrator tells the thoughts of his youth and reprimands God for His lack of constancy and general unreliability:

> ... mais, *je sais aussi que la constance n'a pas fixé, dans tes os, comme une moelle tenace, le harpon de sa demeure éternelle* et que tu retombes assez souvent, toi et tes pensées, recouvertes de la lèpre noire de l'erreur, dans le lac funèbre des sombres malédictions.

(II, 12, pp. 201-202)

The abstract noun *constance* is made concrete and personified by the verb *fixer* which connotes permanence (in this case deficient, since the verb is negative). *Dans tes os* suggests something solid to grasp. The vehicle, however, is ambiguous. If there is an ellipsis, and I think that the reader is likely to view it as one at first sight, we supply *comme dans une moelle tenace.* Then *moelle tenace* is the vehicle for the tenor *os,* and the analogy becomes understandable. [7] In that case the metaphor develops logically. But if there is no ellipsis then the tenor of the comparison is *harpon,* the object of *fixer.* In the first case *moelle* is emphasized, in the second *tenace.* If the second interpretation is correct, the distance between the tenor and the vehicle is greater, and the image is more striking: it is more unusual to think of *harpon* as *moelle tenace* than it is to think of bones as solid marrow. Thus the oxymoron *moelle tenace* can be explained in either direction and prevents us from clearly visualizing the image. But at the same time, it suggests the nature of God's character and represents the main theme of the statement (weakness and tenacity). A traditional image would show us God unable to

---

[7] I am aware that grammarians are wary of the notion of ellipsis. We cannot, however, discount the reader's sensation of an ellipsis in certain cases.

hold a desired moral attribute. Lautréamont reverses the process: *constance,* the attribute, is described in terms of a fisherman (*fixer le harpon*) while God becomes the prey, an object (*retomber dans le lac*). And we would expect *fixer la demeure éternelle de son harpon* since constancy is trying to become fixed, but instead we read *le harpon de sa demeure éternelle.* We can no longer be sure of what is abstract and what is concrete. The normal perception of the world is turned inside out. [8] In this context, the ambiguity of the simile's vehicle, partaking of both the prey (*dans tes os*) and the instrument of attack (*le harpon*), illustrates the unusual angle of presentation.

In the first stanza of Chant III ,the two *frères mystérieux,* Mario and Maldoror, ride their horses high above the earth, and deplore humanity's evil. Maldoror tries to console his brother by pointing out to him that he is still young and that many pleasures await him:

> A mon tour, je m'efforce de lui rappeler *sa jeunesse dorée, qui ne demande qu'à s'avancer dans les palais des plaisirs, comme une reine* ; mais il remarque que mes paroles sortent difficilement de ma bouche amaigrie, et que *les années de mon propre printemps ont passé, tristes et glaciales, comme un rêve implacable qui promène, sur les tables des banquets et sur les lits de satin, où sommeille la pâle prêtresse d'amour,* payée avec les miroitements de l'or, *les voluptés amères du désenchantement, les rides pestilentielles de la vieillesse, les effarements de la solitude* et *les flambeaux de la douleur.*
>
> (III, 1, pp. 223-224)

There seem to be, at first, two separate metaphoric developments, but they are really interwoven and, like the brothers, depend on one another. The first part, glorifying the expectations of youth, has an ascending evolution, while the second part, conjuring up the evils of old age, develops into a downgrading of the tenor of the comparison.

In Maldoror's remark to Mario, the tenor *jeunesse dorée,* although a description of his actual youth, carries with it, nonetheless, the connotation of aristocracy that the phrase usually suggests. The vehicle *comme une reine* suggests regal grandeur. But the tenor is first personified in the subordinate clause by *ne demande qu'à s'avancer.* The metaphor *les palais des plaisirs* juxtaposes the con-

---

[8] For the psychoanalytic significance of the tendency to reverse relationships, see Rispal "Le Monde de Lautréamont", pp. 15-19. The interest of these reversals for the present study, however, is primarily psychological and ontological, i.e. how they affect our perception of the nature of reality.

crete level of *reine* with the abstract level of *jeunesse* and provides a
link for the analogy.

The second part of the sentence is Mario's reply, and it transforms
the original glorification into decay. The tenor *les années de mon
propre printemps* replaces *jeunesse dorée,* and *s'avancer* with its suggestion of progress, has become *ont passé,* in the present past. The
adjectives in apposition, describing *années, tristes et glaciales* reju-
venate the cliché *printemps* (for youth) by continuing the metaphor.
Glaciales, suggesting an unpleasant, cold spring, becomes, in juxtaposition to *tristes,* both literal and figurative. The vehicle of the
second comparison *comme un rêve implacable qui promène* reduces
the hope implied in *s'avancer comme une reine* to an obsessive fantasy, personified by the nonchalant *promène.* But the object of
promène is delayed by a long disjunction which is actually a description of the initial *palais des plaisirs* since it enumerates palatial fur-
nishings: *sur les tables des banquets et sur les lits de satin.* These,
in context, become symbols of decadence. The queen, representing
glory and hope in the first image, now appears as *la pâle prêtresse
d'amour,* a tired (*sommeille*) prostitute (*payée avec les miroitements
de l'or*). Moreover, the nominal construction makes *les miroitements
de l'or* abstract and therefore more difficult to visualize than, for
instance, *de l'or miroitant.* As is, however, the structure presents
another problem for the reader, because it is followed by the object
of *promène,* a series of metaphors which have the same form (noun
and attribute), but which could also be the objects of *payée.* Then
the metaphors would all be the rewards earned by the *pâle prêtresse
d'amour,* an easily conceived development. This would, however, leave
the transitive verb *promène* without an object and the reader realizes
this at the end of the sentence. He is therefore forced to reread in
order to understand the statement. And only after having cleared up,
in his own mind, the syntactical complexity, does he feel the full
impact of the image: an inexorable dream parading all the curses of
old age and disillusion. Again, from our point of view, this is a
reversal since we are more likely to think of old age as trying not
to give up a dream.

In the objects themselves, the abstract nouns (*désenchantement,
vieillesse, solitude, douleur*) are made concrete, in each case, by a
pejorative focus which is either concrete by nature (*les rides pestilen-
tielles, les flambeaux*), by an adjective (*les voluptés amères*), or by
the plural (*les effarements*). Although these metaphors are relatively

strong, they are not too unexpected as emblematic symbols of decre-
pitude. Their intensity is due, not so much to their originality, as to
their accumulation and their parallelism.

Thus, the second part of the sentence amplifies the original
pleasing and hopeful image, converting it into a pessimistic and
discouraging vision, by a series of antithetical specifics. In the process, the vehicles of the similes, though an essential part of the image,
are submerged in the overall metaphoric development and the reader
has a tendency to lose sight of them.

In the example we have just analyzed, we are given an illustration
of both aspects of aging. The paradoxical nature of the theme
requires an abrupt reversal, hence the separation into two distinct
parts. The following example, dealing with the replacement of a
virtue by a vice, has a simultaneous development of opposing currents.
God has appeared to Maldoror and reproaches him his ingratitude:

> Maintenant, tu rejettes à tes pieds, comme un haillon souillé de
> boue, la longanimité dont j'ai trop longtemps fait preuve. La
> reconnaissance a vu ses racines se dessécher, comme le lit d'une
> mare ; mais à sa place l'ambition a crû dans des proportions
> qu'il me serait pénible de qualifier.
>
> (V, 4, p. 300)

The three abstract nouns (*la longanimité, la reconnaissance, l'ambition*) represent the moral evolution of Maldoror's relationship to
God and, from God's point of view, the change is a deterioration.
Each abstract noun is made concrete by a focus which expresses the
moral attribute's transformation: patience has been thrown to the
ground, gratitude has dried up and ambition has grown. *La reconnaissance* takes the form of a tree through the focus *ses racines* and
the vehicle of that particular simile *comme le lit d'une mare* echoes
the vehicle of the previous simile *comme un haillon souillé de boue,*
since both vehicles suggest muddiness. The third focus continues the
tree image through the verb *croître,* although it is now a new plant
(*mais à sa place*). But the vehicle, this time, expresses the idea of
indescribably great by stating the impossibility of a concrete representation (*dans des proportions qu'il me serait pénible de qualifier*).
This not only creates a hyperbolic effect but also provides a contrast
for the other two vehicles' topic of earthly matter.

While the abstract level follows a downward path, the figurative
concrete level expresses the notion of growth. The image is remarkable because it combines three metaphors whose frame and focus

evolve in opposite directions yet achieve a unified vision: for the idea
that gratitude is replaced by ambition, we are given the image of
one plant dying while another grows, in its place, to extreme height.

The relatively complex structure of metaphor-simile combinations
yields images whose effect is to put into question the reader's concept
of the nature of reality. Characteristic of these images is their reversal
of normal perception. Even such a common device as the clarification
of a metaphor by the vehicle of a simile can produce a dissolution
of established connotations (the God/Devil reversal in my first
example).

In cases where the vehicle in a simile is metaphoric, the result is
a blurring of the division between the abstract and the concrete (the
first example in the second category), or a lack of parallelism between
the figurative and literal levels (the second example).

Where the simile is part of a general metaphoric development, the
reversal of literal and figurative levels is most apparent. What the
reader would expect to be literal is figurative, and vice-versa. It is
because of such images, I suspect, that the surrealists became aware
of the possibility of breaking down the boundary between reality and
imagination by changing the traditionally accepted ways of using
words:

> Il s'agissait... d'étudier d'aussi près que possible les réactions
> des mots les uns sur les autres. Ce n'est qu'à ce prix qu'on pou-
> vait espérer rendre au langage sa destination pleine, ce qui,
> pour quelques-uns dont j'étais, devait faire faire un grand pas
> à la connaissance, exalter d'autant la vie. Nous nous exposions
> par là aux persécutions d'usage, dans un domaine où le bien
> (bien parler) consiste à tenir compte avant tout de l'étymologie
> du mot, c'est-à-dire de son poids le plus mort, à conformer la
> phrase à une syntaxe médiocrement utilitaire, toutes choses en
> accord avec le piètre conservatisme humain et avec cette hor-
> reur de l'infini qui ne manque pas chez mes semblables une
> occasion de se manifester.... Enfin même le sens des mots ne va
> pas sans mélange et l'on n'est pas près de déterminer dans
> quelle mesure le sens figuré agit progressivement sur le sens
> propre, à chaque variation de celui-ci devant correspondre une
> variation de celui-là. [9]

---

[9] André Breton, "Les Mots sans rides" in *Les Pas Perdus* (Gallimard, 1924),
pp. 167-169.

CHAPTER VI

METAPHORS

"Besides being discussed from the point of view of the symbolism involved, metaphor may be considered from the point of view of the listener. *Here its outstanding characteristic is the sort of shock which it produces,*" writes Paul Henle. "Ordinarily one takes words in their literal sense and this is impossible in a metaphor. This impossibility in fact is what drives one on to seek a figurative meaning." [1] All metaphors are, therefore, striking in some measure. When it becomes possible to read all the words in a metaphoric statement literally, we have a dead metaphor: *the hood of a car* is no longer felt as a metaphor because *hood* has lost its figurative meaning.

However, the shocks, which metaphors produce, vary. There may be a shock of recognition (when an unsuspected similarity is revealed) or a shock of non-recognition (where the reader must attempt to visualize something which has no relation to perceivable reality).

Traditional metaphors are of the recognition type. Since they are mimetic, the reader is able, through a certain amount of mental effort, to understand the image created by the interaction of the frame and the focus. Thus, in Aristotle's example, we can see that evening is "the old age of the day," or that old age is the "sunset of life" because "as old age is to life, so evening is to day." [2] In extended metaphors, such as Donne's famous comparison of the two lovers to twin compasses, this principle can be developed logically point by point. [3] In this case, recognition increases as the analogy becomes more clearly defined.

---

[1] Paul Henle, *Language, Thought and Culture,* p. 182. The italics are mine.

[2] Aristotle, *Rhetoric and Poetics,* trans. by I. Bywater (Modern Library, 1954, p. 252.

[3] John Donne, *A Valediction: Forbidding Mourning,* V, 25-36.

A non-recognition metaphor, on the other hand, produces an image which will remain logically unintelligible, no matter how great an effort is put into the decoding process. The degree of unintelligibility is, of course, variable. Simple lack of recognition may be the result of a reversal of normal perception or because of a mixed (multiple focus) metaphor, which puts into question existing forms, or because it is difficult to determine which words are used figuratively and which are used literally. [4] The more extreme cases, however, do not even permit this kind of awareness, i.e., the clear evaluation of what is wrong, and are therefore classified as visions or hallucinations. This type of image can be found, not only in the surrealists, who consciously sought to create it, [5] but also among poets who are generally considered visionaries, from the so-called baroque writers of the beginning of the seventeenth century to those of the end of the nineteenth century. Here are some examples: "J'écoute à demi transporté / Le bruit des ailes du silence / Qui vole dans l'obscurité" (Saint-Amant), [6] "Satan rit et cracha du côté du tonnerre / *L'immensité,* qu'emplit l'ombre visionnaire, / *Frissonna.* Ce crachat fut plus tard Barabbas" (Hugo), [7] "Et des cataractes pesantes, / Comme des rideaux de cristal, / Se suspendaient, éblouissantes, / A des murailles de métal" (Baudelaire), [8] "Le pavillon en viande saignante sur la soie des mers et des fleurs arctiques; (elles n'existent pas)" (Rimbaud). [9]

From Saint-Amant's metaphor which requires an adjustment of perception, to Rimbaud's image in which the signifiers have no realistic referent, the reader is unable to rely on sense experience and must imagine something which has no counterpart in everyday reality.

An affective approach to the metaphors in *Les Chants de Maldoror* has to classify them according to these two extremes: from the rela-

---

[4] An example of the normative objections to this type of image can be found in Antoine Albalat, *Comment il ne faut pas écrire* (Paris, 1921) under the heading "Les images forcées," pp. 89-92. Images are bad because they are not logical: "Le défaut ordinaire des comparaisons et des images, c'est leur manque de logique" (p. 89); and because they do not conform to scientific truth: "Il y a des écrivains qui, pour trouver une image, inventeraient la physiologie et la botanique." (p. 89).

[5] See Breton's classification and examples in the first *Manifeste du surréalisme* (Paris, 1924, reprinted in *Manifeste du surréalisme* (Paris: Gallimard, 1963), pp. 52-53, and Balakian, *Surrealism,* pp. 120-140.

[6] Saint-Amant, "Le Contemplateur" in *Œuvres* (Jannet), p. 37.

[7] Hugo, "Et nox facta est" in *La Fin de Satan* (ed. La Pléiade), p. 767.

[8] Baudelaire, "Rêve parisien" in *Les Fleurs du Mal* (Garnier), p. 114.

[9] Rimbaud, "Barbare" in *Illuminations* (La Pléiade), p. 198.

tively mild shock of recognition to the brutal shock of non-recognition. I have therefore proceeded, by degree, from conventional metaphors, based on analogy, to the ones which, in Anna Balakian's words, "are derived from divergence and contradiction." [10]

If we consider a metaphor as it is written, that is, as a statement which cannot be read literally, we find that, out of four theoretical possibilities, there are only two actual combinations: 1) A concrete focus in an abstract frame. The word which is used figuratively is concrete and therefore concretizes an abstract word which is used literally (*the flow of time*). Through overuse this type of metaphor becomes a cliché, but because of the difference in word class, it cannot become literal, i.e., a dead metaphor. 2) A concrete focus in a concrete frame. Both the figurative word and the literal context are concrete (*the crest of a mountain*). Because of the identical word class, this type of metaphor may become literal and die out.

It would also be possible, in theory, to have an abstract focus in a concrete frame, but I have not found any examples where an abstract word is used figuratively in a literal context. [11] Even in the case of allegories (the concretization of an abstraction), the concrete level is still the focus, since it is an extended figurative development.

The fourth combination (an abstract focus in an abstract frame) presents a statement which cannot be perceived by the senses and can consequently not be considered an image.

1) A concrete focus in an abstract frame.

a) Clichés.

A cliché, unlike a dead metaphor, can be a striking device because it is recognizable as such and I do not imply any value judgment as to its effectiveness as a unit. [12] But it is not remarkable as a metaphor since the reader no longer senses the distance between the two terms

---

[10] Balakian, *Surrealism,* p. 120.

[11] In similes, it may happen that there is a concrete tenor with an abstract vehicle because both terms of the comparison are literal. Stephen Ullmann gives these examples: "La lune, froide et claire comme un doute, Sourit et passe" from Viélé-Griffin, and "Et nous, jaillis de plus loin comme un aveu plus hardi" from Jules Romains. "L'image littéraire," p. 52.

[12] For the stylistic value of clichés, see Michael Riffaterre, "Fonctions du cliché dans la prose littéraire," *CAIEF* (March 1964), pp. 81-85.

"Cette unité linguistique [the cliché] est expressive, puisqu'elle provoque des réactions esthétiques, morales ou affectives. Elle est d'ordre structural, et non sémantique, puisqu'une substitution synonymique efface le cliché. Elle

of the metaphoric statement . The cliché produces the weakest shock effect because it does not present any difficulty in decoding and because it does not reveal an unsuspected relationship. I shall, however, point out cases where the use of a cliché seems particularly significant.

In Chant II, stanza 3, the poet complains about God's apparent indifference to human suffering, and sarcastically explains His haughtiness:

> Mais, il [Dieu] est grand et noble ; il l'emporte sur nous par la puissance de ses conceptions ; s'il parlementait avec les hommes *toutes les hontes rejailliraient jusqu'à son visage.*
>
> (II, 3, p. 166)

Rejaillir is commonly used with shame or honor (*l'honneur en rejaillit sur lui*). This usage seems to go at least as far back as Racine: "Et pourquoi me cacher? et par quelle injustice / Faut-il que sur mon front sa honte rejaillisse?" [13]

In the previous stanza, as the poet was about to begin writing, a storm broke out and thunder struck him. But the wound heals rapidly, and he urges Léman not to be frightened by the scar:

> ... sinon je croirais que tu n'as pas le courage de contempler, avec sang-froid, la grande balafre occasionnée par un supplice déjà perdu pour moi dans *la nuit des temps passés.*
>
> (II, 2, p. 165)

And the poet, in spite of the difficulty of writing, and the warning from above, decides that he must continue:

> N'importe ; j'aurai cependant la force de soulever le porte-plume, et le courage de *creuser ma pensée.*
>
> (II, 2, p. 165)

An indication that a metaphor is a cliché is its renewal in other contexts. Thus, *la nuit des temps* is used by La Fontaine, as the

---

n'admet pas de variantes.   Elle a la même facilité de substitution et de distribution qu'un mot.

"Il s'agit donc bien d'une structure de style, puisqu'elle attire l'attention sur la forme du message linguistique. Mais c'est une structure unique en ceci que son contenu lexical est déjà en place; un cadre vide passe partout et peut organiser n'importe quel contexte; mais un cadre déjà rempli sera toujours senti comme un emprunt, toujours en contraste avec le contexte où il est importé." (p. 82.)

[13] Racine, "Iphigénie," III, 2, in *Théâtre complet* (Garnier), p. 503.

frame of another metaphor: "Puisse le tout, ô charmante Philis, / Aller si loin que notre los franchisse / La nuit des temps ! nous la saurons dompter. / Moi par écrire, et vous par réciter." [14]; likewise, by Baudelaire: "... sentiments et ... pensées poétiques déjà connus, mais qu'on croyait enfouis dans la nuit du passé." [15] In the context of my example from Lautréamont, however, *la nuit des temps passés,* although intact as a cliché, appears as an exaggeration because the speaker has just been wounded. It emphasizes the supernatural rapidity with which Maldoror heals. The use of *creuser sa pensée,* in my second example, is less effective, since it seems ready-made for the context. Flaubert renews it by building another metaphor on it *(aviron/plume, idée/courant)*: "Quel lourd aviron qu'une plume et combien l'idée quand il la faut creuser avec, est un dur courant." [16]

In the first of the family scenes where the hero, like an evil spirit, makes his presence felt, there is an anticipation of doom in the air:

> La fin de cette veillée ne se passera pas sans que quelque événement funeste nous *plonge* tous les trois *dans le lac du désespoir.*
>
> (I, 11, p. 145)

The metaphors *un lac d'amertume* or *un lac d'oubli* are commonly used. [17] In context (it is either the father or the mother speaking), the cliché is indicative of the conventional literary speech pattern and underlines the artificiality of the situation. Lautréamont uses a similar metaphor in a different context, [18] but renews the cliché by adding, to both the focus and the frame, an adjective which emphasizes the connotations:

> ... tu retombes [Dieu] assez souvent, toi et tes pensées, recouvertes de la lèpre noire de l'erreur, dans *le lac funèbre des sombres malédictions.*
>
> (II, 12, pp. 201-202)

The cliché is, moreover, rejuvenated by the substitution of *malédictions* which has more emotive power than *amertume, oubli* or

---

[14] La Fontaine, *Fables, contes et nouvelles* (La Pléiade), p. 642.

[15] Baudelaire, *Curiosités esthétiques,* XVX, I (La Pléiade), p. 857.

[16] Flaubert, *Correspondance,* II (Charpentier), p. 62.

[17] The *Robert* lists them among the figurative uses of *lac* and the *Larousse du XIXe siècle* gives this example from Henri Cantel: "J'aime! et pourtant l'amour qui doit être une joie / Est un lac d'amertume dont l'eau s'est enfuie."

[18] See Chapter V, above.

désespoir and whose plural form makes it more concrete than the customary abstract frame.

In the ocean stanza, Lautréamont compares the irrational behavior of human beings to the stability of the ocean:

> Qui comprendra pourquoi deux amants qui s'idolâtraient la veille, pour un mot mal interprété, s'écartent l'un vers l'orient, l'autre vers l'occident, avec *les aiguillons de la haine, de la vengeance, de l'amour et du remords,* et ne se revoient plus...
>
> (I, 9, p. 139)

Aiguillons is often used figuratively with strong emotions. I have found this example in Anatole France: "Vous y auriez vu que, dans une solitude affreuse, loin de toute figure taillée ou peinte, déchirés par le cilice, macérés par la pénitence, épuisés par le jeûne, se roulant sur un lit d'épines, les anachorètes se sentaient percés jusqu'aux moelles des *aiguillons du désir charnel.*" [19] In Lautréamont's case, however, the accumulation of frames renews the cliché by calling attention to the figurative use of *aiguillons,* since the reader has to supply the focus in all but the initial frame. Furthermore, in the context of *Les Chants'* aggressive content, a word like *aiguillons,* even when used in a cliché, is striking because it is a key word, indicative of a thematic pattern.

b) The metaphor is original but mimetic.

Whether or not a metaphor is original depends, of course, on the reader's general culture. To lessen subjectivity, I have verified my own impressions in Paul Robert's *Dictionnaire alphabétique et analogique de la langue française,* which gives word associations as well as literal meanings, and in the *Larousse du XXe siècle.* The procedure consisted in eliminating from this classification all cases where identical or similar figurative word usages could be found. This method does not guarantee a metaphor's originality, but it avoids total reliance on personal experience and, until there is more statistical data on the subject, seems to be the most practical way of coping with the problem.

A metaphor is mimetic when all or some of the connotations of the focus are logically consistent with the denotation of the frame.

---

[19] Anatole France, *Les Opinions de M. Jérôme Coignard* (Calmann-Lévy, 1923), p. 208.

The meaning of the word which is used literally determines which associations of the word used figuratively are valid in the particular context. Thus, when words enter into a metaphorical relationship with each other, they mutually limit their meanings. For example, in the statement *the frontiers of knowledge,* the word *frontiers* suggests attained limits beyond which there is the unknown, and knowledge becomes a finite area.

In the first group of these metaphors, the image is expressive of a thematic development. It serves to give a vivid and concrete representation of an idea. In the family scene in Chant I, while Maldoror is tempting the child, the father is praying:

> Si quelque pensée orgueilleuse, s'insinue dans notre imagination, nous la rejetons aussitôt avec *la salive du dédain* et nous t'en faisons le sacrifice irrémissible.

> (I, 11, p. 149)

In this highly stylized situation,[20] the metaphor *la salive du dédain,* because of the vulgar associations of the focus, calls attention to itself and suggests, because it is overly emotive, that the speaker's humility is feigned. This enables the reader to sense Lautréamont's ironic view of the scene and reminds him that the atmosphere of impending doom is only fiction.

The narrator and Mario, "le génie de la terre et le génie de la mer" (p. 221), are galloping along the seashore. Maldoror has been trying in vain to console his brother who bemoans the human condition. He cannot speak because the horses might understand him and knowledge might lead to their downfall as it has led to mankind's:

> En effet, ne pense qu'*aux marcassins de l'humanité* : le degré d'intelligence qui les sépare des autres êtres de la création ne semble-t-il pas ne leur être accordé qu'au prix irrémédiable de souffrances incalculables ?

> (III, 1, p. 226)

Since *marcassins* are small wild boars, the figurative use of the word suggests pettiness and moral degradation. In context, the topic

---

[20] A stylized passage is one where the reader senses the borrowing of a convention from another literary genre. The transposition into a different context produces a contrast with the pattern, and acts then as an ironic device.

It has been suggested that the family scenes in *Les Chants de Maldoror* are parodies of the Comtesse de Ségur. See Marcel Jean and Arpad Mezei, *Maldoror,* pp. 65-66.

being animal intelligence, it serves to dehumanize humanity, to emphasize that man is just another animal species, whose difference in degree of intelligence doesn't seem worth all his sufferings. By contrast, La Fontaine uses the adjectival form of the same word, in a literal sense, to humanize the animal: "La faim détruisit tout: il ne resta personne / De la gent marcassine et de la gent aiglonne." [21]

A toad who, thanks to Maldoror, has become more intelligent and is able to speak to him, deplores the hero's evil behavior and urges him to leave this world:

> De quel droit viens-tu sur cette terre, pour tourner en dérision ceux qui l'habitent, *épave pourrie, ballottée par le septicisme*?
>
> (I, 13, p. 159)

The word *épave* is used figuratively for a person without will power who is physically and morally degraded (Cf. Baudelaire's *Les Epaves*). This connotation is reinforced by the insulting adjective *pourrie*. The verbal adjective in apposition *ballottée* continues the ship metaphor in an expected manner—Lautréamont uses the same combination (*ballotte/épave*) in a comparison of his own fatigue to that of a shipwrecked man on a raft: "... si la lame le ballotte, comme une épave, pendant des heures plus prolongée que la vie d'homme..." (p. 271). But here *ballotte* is used literally. By using it as a focus, in the example above, the frame *le scepticisme,* an attitude often associated with wisdom, acquires pejorative connotations. The image is striking since the implications of one of its members are changed.

At the end of the stanza which tells of the happy metamorphosis into a *pourceau,* Maldoror wakes up and realizes that it was only a dream:

> Il est temps de quitter ces souvenirs glorieux, qui ne laissent après leur suite que *la pâle voie lactée des regrets éternels.*
>
> (IV, 6, p. 274)

For the reader, the metamorphosis into a pig would seem repulsive. Because Homer uses the reader's normal associations, the transformation of Ulysses' men, by Circe, into pigs, is morally and physically downgrading. Throughout the stanza, Lautréamont's development has reversed the consecrated symbolism of the pig, by a lyrical description of the change. Immediately preceding my exam-

---

[21] La Fontaine, *Fables, contes et nouvelles* (La Pléiade), p. 79.

ple, he writes: "Combien de fois, depuis cette nuit passée à la belle étoile sur une falaise, ne me suis-je pas mêlé à des troupeaux de pourceaux, pour reprendre, comme un droit, ma métamorphose détruite!" Yet, the metaphor, which ends the last sentence in the stanza, casts doubt on the earnestness of the proclaimed enthusiasm: the focus *la pâle voie lactée* seems overly romantic, and emphasizes the hyperbolic quality of *ces souvenirs glorieux* and of the frame *regrets éternels*. This convergence of exaggerations gives the impression of irony which, in turn, disrupts the pattern of emotional intensity set by the context.

While the first examples in this category are remarkable because they are expressive elements in their immediate context, the second group of metaphors is striking because they deal with recurring themes in *Les Chants de Maldoror*.

The grave-digger, whom Maldoror is helping, tries to determine the identity of the stranger:

> Quoiqu'il dise ce qu'il ne pense pas, je crois néanmoins qu'il a des raisons pour agir comme il l'a fait, *excité par les restes en lambeaux d'une charité détruite en lui.*
>
> (I, 12, p. 154)

The theme of tearing and of shreds runs all through the first Chant. In the stanza on how to torture a child, Lautréamont says, "Bande-lui les yeux pendant que tu déchireras ses chairs palpitantes" (p. 128), but it will be a reciprocal tearing: "Alors, tu [the adolescent] me déchireras sans jamais t'arrêter, avec les dents et les ongles à la fois... et nous souffrirons tous les deux, moi, d'être déchiré, toi, de me déchirer..." (p. 129), and in the barking dogs episode: "Après quelques heures, les chiens... se précipitent les uns sur les autres, sans savoir ce qu'ils font, et se déchirent en mille lambeaux, avec une rapidité incroyable" (p. 133) and "dans un désespoir qui m'enivre comme le vin, je meurtris de mes puissantes mains ma poitrine en lambeaux" (p. 135). [22]

Blanchot remarks that Maldoror never seems to commit an act of cruelty without immediately feeling remorse and identifying with

---

[22] Yvonne Rispal, "Le Monde de Lautréamont," pp. 22-23, points out that while *déchirer* is predominant in Chant I, *toucher* becomes the main verb of sense perception in Chant VI. She interprets this as a significant change in personality : "Ainsi deux simples mots, 'déchirer' et 'toucher', mettent à jour un problème affectif très grave, puisqu'il intéresse toute la sensibilité ducassienne recevant la sensation comme une blessure, une sorte d'agression" (p. 23).

the victim: "Puis, remontant des scènes aux détails, des épisodes aux images [in a thematic analysis], l'on verrait qu'à côté des mouvements de plaisir que lui donne le mal qu'il fait à autrui, Maldoror exprime presque toujours un sentiment de malaise moral, un regret, un repentir honteux ou une bizarre soif de pardon.... Il est donc aussi bien celui qui est blessé que celui qui blesse. Le sang qui coule lui rappelle son propre sang, les larmes qu'il fait verser ont le goût de ses larmes. Qui est la victime ? Qui est le bourreau ? L'ambiguïté est parfaite." [23]

The image in the above example summarizes this ambiguity: *excité par les restes en lambeaux* expresses the sadistic pleasure which shreds give to Maldoror and *une charité détruite en lui* justifies his lack of compassion by implying that others are to blame for it. At the same time, however, there is a suggestion of masochism due to the fact that Maldoror is excited by his own figurative shreds.

The madwoman, whose daughter was raped and mutilated by the hero and his bulldog, is being persecuted by children:

> Elle va devant soi, comme la feuille du peuplier, emportée, elle, sa jeunesse, ses illusions et son bonheur passé, qu'elle revoit à travers *les brumes d'une intelligence détruite par le tourbillon des facultés inconscientes.*
>
> (III, 22, p. 227)

The focus *les brumes* is not unusual in reference to ideas which lack clarity. I found this example from Jules Renard: "Réalisme, idéalisme, autant de brumes à travers lesquelles l'homme aveugle cherche la vérité." [24] Likewise, *tourbillon* is used figuratively for thoughts which rapidly succeed each other, as in Léon Bloy: "Je suis monté un jour d'orage, dans la pluie furieuse, dans l'effort des vents enragés, dans l'ouragan de mon espoir et le tourbillon de mes pensées." [25] In Lautréamont, this use is more significant, since *tourbillon* is a key word, recurring often as part of the leitmotif of narcissistic circularity. For instance: "Je pourrais... te saisir par les jambes, te faire rouler autour de moi, comme une fronde, concentrer mes forces en décrivant la dernière circonférence, et te lancer contre la muraille." (p. 173), and in the Falmer episode: "... je le saisis par les cheveux avec un bras de fer, et le fis tournoyer dans l'air avec une telle vitesse,

[23] Maurice Blanchot, *Lautréamont et Sade*, p. 263.
[24] Renard, *Journal* (N.R.F.), p. 543.
[25] Léon Bloy, *La Femme Pauvre* (Mercure de France, 1937), p. 76.

que la chevelure me resta dans la main." (p. 182). Maldoror also uses the same type of motion in the story of the murder of Mervyn (pp. 357-358). Paul Zweig, in his discussion of this theme, points out that "L'art de la parole, la violence, le jeu des facultés inconscientes: tous sont emportés dans un mouvement 'giratoire' par ce 'tourbillon', qui imprime son énergie à toute l'œuvre." [26]

c) Continued metaphors.

Maldoror is telling a passing traveler not to stop, for it would weaken his courage:

> Laisse-moi réchauffer ma ténacité à la flamme du martyre volontaire.
>
> (IV, 4, p. 266)

The first focus, *réchauffer,* is common with qualities which are weakening. For example, in Racine: "Il [Néron] veut que d'un festin la pompe et l'allégresse / Confirmant à leurs yeux la foi de nos serments, / Et réchauffent l'ardeur de nos embrassements; /." [27] The second focus *la flamme* is used in everyday language with emotions or ideals: *la flamme de l'enthousiasme, de l'idéal.* But the image is striking because the second focus continues the first and thus unifies two separate abstractions by making them part of a single metaphoric statement.

A similar effect is produced by the following example from the self-description stanza in Chant VI ("Je me suis aperçu que je n'avais qu'un œil au milieu du front"):

> Je n'envie rien au Créateur ; mais qu'il me laisse descendre le fleuve de ma destinée à travers une série croissante de crimes glorieux.
>
> (VI, IV, p. 340)

The figurative use of *le fleuve* is a cliché (*le fleuve de la vie*). As the direct object of *descendre,* however, it conveys the idea that destiny is a descent rather than an ascent. Likewise, *une série croissante* is a cliché, but as a focus for *crimes glorieux,* it reinforces the honorific connotations of the frame. Moreover, it continues *descendre le fleuve* by antithesis. This gives an impression of parallelism and makes *crimes glorieux* synonymous with *ma destinée.*

---

[26] Paul Zweig, "Lautréamont, ou les violences du Narcisse," pp. 11-12.
[27] Racine, "Britannicus," V, 1, in *Théâtre complet* (Garnier), p. 284.

In Chant II, Lautréamont tells of his childhood and his original innocence:

> Mais non, je savais de reste que *les roses heureuses de l'ado-lescence ne devaient pas fleurir perpétuellement tressées en guirlandes capricieuses, sur son front modeste et noble,* qu'em-brassaient avec frénésie toutes les mères.
>
> (II, 8, p. 182)

The cliché (Cf. Ronsard's " Cueillez dès aujourd'hui les roses de la vie") is renewed by the continuation of the metaphor (*fleurir... tressées en guirlandes*). At the same time, the qualifying adjectives *heureuses* and *capricieuses,* and the adverb *perpétuellement* make the statement seem hyperbolic.   In this context, *son front modeste et noble* becomes mocking rather than flattering while *avec frénésie* suggests that the mothers have ulterior motives. The effect is ironic and the scene acquires an aura of theatricality which disrupts the sincere tone of the beginning of the stanza (*On raconte que je naquis entre les bras de la surdité*). This prevents the reader from deter-mining whether the story is a realistic autobiography or an imaginary childhood based on literary commonplaces.

d) Metaphors continued with multiple focus. [28]

Throughout the mathematics stanza (II, 10), there are three main figurative levels: 1) mathematics as teacher, 2) mathematics as life-giving force and 3) mathematics as religion (architecture, revelation, God, etc.). Because this metaphoric development is very long (over four pages) it was necessary at times to paraphrase or quote the content. This is purely to indicate the continuity and is not meant to be a substitute for analysis. The stanza begins with the teacher theme:

> O mathématiques sévères, je ne vous ai pas oubliées, depuis que vos savantes leçons, plus douces que le miel, filtrèrent dans mon cœur, comme une onde rafraîchissante.
>
> (II, 10, p. 190)

The adjective *sévères* introduces the suggestion of authority which becomes more markedly instructive with *savantes leçons.* This serves as tenor for the presentation of the pleasant and nourishing aspect of

---

[28] I call *multiple focus* metaphors those which are usually referred to as *mixed* metaphors, in order to avoid the pejorative connotations of the latter term.

mathematics: *plus douces que le miel.* The verbal focus *filtrèrent,* suggesting purification, acts as tenor for the vehicle *comme une onde rafraîchissante* which has associations of rejuvenation. The second sentence continues the water image:

> J'aspirais instinctivement, dès le berceau, à boire à votre source, plus ancienne que le soleil ; et je continue encore de fouler le parvis sacré de votre temple solennel, moi, le plus fidèle de vos initiés.
>
> (II, 10, p. 190)

The first part of the statement repeats the structure of the initial comparison in the opening sentence, but shifts to a different figurative level: *votre source, plus ancienne que le soleil* is parallel to *vos savantes leçons, plus douces que le miel.* Then, after the conjunction *et,* the development changes to the mystical metaphor with the focus *fouler le parvis sacré de votre temple solennel* which is continued by *moi, le plus fidèle de vos initiés.* Thus, from the very beginning of the stanza, the three main themes are simultaneously presented.

The poet then proceeds to relate the benefits of his contact with mathematics:

> Il y avait du vague dans mon esprit, un je ne sais quoi épais comme la fumée ; mais je sus franchir religieusement les degrés qui mènent à votre autel, et vous avez chassé ce voile obscur, comme le vent chasse le damier.
>
> (II, 10, p. 190)

The idea of vagueness in the narrator's mind is conveyed by the renewal of the cliché *un je ne sais quoi* through the simile in apposition *épais comme la fumée.* This is the frame for the focus *ce voile obscur,* while the religion image is continued from the previous sentence with *je sus franchir religieusement les degrés qui mènent à votre autel.* The last simile, *vous avez chassé ce voile obscur, comme le vent chasse le damier* is, however, disruptive. The analogies *les mathématiques/le vent* and *ce voile obscur/le damier* are unexpected because they reverse the reader's associations: *le vent,* being sensual rather than visual, is in the line of development of *la fumée* and *ce voile obscur* while *le damier* makes the vagueness theme abruptly concrete. An expected comparison would have been something more tangible chasing something less visual. The reader is forced to reread in order to make certain that he understands Lautréamont's analogy, and the disruptive element becomes an attention provoking device.

Next, vagueness is replaced by clear understanding:

> A l'aide de votre lait fortifiant, mon intelligence s'est rapide-
> ment développée, et a pris des proportions immenses, au milieu
> de cette clarté ravissante dont vous faites présent, avec prodi-
> galité à ceux qui vous aiment d'un sincère amour.
>
> (II, 10, p. 191)

The energy-giving theme is resumed by the focus *votre lait forti-
fiant,* which also suggests motherhood. This connotation is reinforced by the personification and growth theme of *mon intelligence
s'est rapidement développée, et a pris des proportions immenses.*
That is followed by a return to the religion and worshipper analogy:
*au milieu de cette clarté ravissante dont vous faites présent, avec
prodigalité à ceux qui vous aiment d'un sincère amour.* In line with
this development, the three branches of mathematics become the
trinity:

> Arithmétique ! algèbre ! géométrie ! trinité grandiose ! triangle
> lumineux !
>
> (II, 10, p. 191)

Consequently, someone who is ignorant of mathematics is a heretic
and deserves torture: "Celui qui ne vous a pas connues est un
insensé! Il mériterait l'épreuve des plus grands supplices; car il y a
du mépris aveugle dans son insouciante ignorance..." while the ini-
tiated is given spiritual strength through their power:

> ... mais celui qui vous connaît et vous apprécie ne veut plus
> rien des biens de la terre ; se contente de vos jouissances
> magiques ; et porté sur vos ailes sombres, ne désire plus que
> de s'élever, d'un vol léger, en construisant une hélice ascen-
> dante, vers la voûte sphérique des cieux.
>
> (II, 10, p. 191)

Since the topic now is the freedom which mathematics give to
those who know them, the shift to a bird metaphor with *vos ailes
sombres* is not surprising, although *sombres* suggests that the freedom
is not easily achieved. But the end of the sentence disrupts the
poetic pattern by abruptly changing to scientific language (*en cons-
truisant une hélice ascendante*). This sudden deviation calls the
reader's attention to the leitmotif of circularity, whose rising motion
leads to heaven (*vers la voûte sphérique des cieux*), that is to say, to
the absolute.

By contrast, earthly reality offers nothing but false truth:

> La terre ne lui montre que des illusions et des fantasmagories
> morales ; mais vous, Ô mathématiques concises, par l'enchaî-
> nement rigoureux de vos propositions tenaces, et la constance
> de vos lois de fer, vous faites luire, aux yeux éblouis, un reflet
> puissant de cette vérité suprême dont on remarque l'empreinte
> dans l'ordre de l'univers.
>
> (II, 10, p. 191)

The opposition is marked by the division of the sentence into two
parts, separated by the semicolon. In the first part, the earth is
downgraded by the restrictive *ne ... que* and by the pejorative *illu-
sions* and *fantasmagories morales*. The second part of the sentence,
beginning with the conjunction of opposition *mais*, returns to the
direct address with the invocation *O mathématiques*, and then emphasizes the contrasting solidity of mathematics through the epithets
concises, rigoureux, tenaces, and through *la constance de vos lois de
fer*. The end of the sentence, to convey the idea that the order of
the universe is but an approximation of real order, contrasts the illu-
minating power of mathematics (*vous faites luire, aux yeux éblouis,
un reflet puissant*) with their faint manifestation in the world (*dont
on remarque l'empreinte dans l'ordre de l'univers*). Mathematics,
therefore, represent the true creation:

> Mais l'ordre qui vous entoure, représenté surtout par la régu-
> larité parfaite du carré, l'ami de Pythagore, est encore plus
> grand ; car le Tout-Puissant, s'est révélé complètement, lui et
> ses attributs, dans ce travail mémorable qui consista à faire
> sortir des entrailles du chaos, vos trésors de théorèmes et vos
> magnifiques splendeurs.
>
> (II, 10, p. 191)

To suggest that mathematics are the real order of the universe,
Lautréamont refers to them now in terms associated with Creation:
*le Tout-Puissant, s'est révélé complètement, lui et ses attributs, ce
travail mémorable* and *faire sortir des entrailles du chaos*. And the
subsequent development implies that they are a much more permanent
world than the human one:

> Aux époques antiques et dans les temps modernes, plus d'une
> grande imagination humaine vit son génie épouvanté, à la
> contemplation de vos figures symboliques tracées sur le papier
> brûlant, comme autant de signes mystérieux, vivants d'une
> haleine latente, que ne comprend pas le vulgaire profane et qui

n'étaient que la révélation éclatante d'axiomes et d'hiéroglyphes
éternels, qui ont existé avant l'univers et qui se maintiendront
après lui.

(II, 10, p. 191)

The religion/worshipper analogy is continued by the personification of human imagination (*vit son génie épouvanté*), which places it
in the role of someone who contemplates the symbols of mathematics
as if they were mystical signs: *vos figures symboliques tracées sur
le papier brûlant, comme autant de signes mystérieux, vivants d'une
haleine latente.* The magical power of these symbols is suggested
by the adjectives *brûlant* and *mystérieux,* by the vehicle of the simile,
and by the subordinate clause *que ne comprend pas le vulgaire
profane,* while the end of the sentence emphasizes the transcendental
significance of the figures (*et qui n'étaient que la révélation éclatante
d'axiomes et d'hiéroglyphes éternels qui ont existé avant l'univers et
qui se maintiendront après lui*). Hence, the human mind will remain
in awe before this divine image:

> Il [the human mind] incline ses genoux devant vous, et sa
> vénération rend hommage à votre visage divin, comme à la
> propre image du Tout-Puissant.
>
> (II, 10, p. 192)

The stanza had begun by comparing mathematics to a religious
edifice, but as the development progressed it shifted towards an actual
identification of mathematics with God, so that, in the above example,
they acquire a *visage divin.* And the vehicle *comme à la propre
image du Tout-Puissant,* instead of merely creating another comparison, reinforces the suggestion of equality of mathematics and God.

Having established this fusion, the poet relates his personal encounter with the three branches of mathematics:

> Pendant mon enfance, vous m'apparûtes une nuit de mai, aux
> rayons de la lune, sur une prairie verdoyante, au bord d'un
> ruisseau limpide, toutes les trois égales en grâce et en pudeur,
> toutes les trois pleines de majesté comme des reines.
>
> (II, 10, p. 192)

An idyllic setting is created by the accumulation of poetic commonplaces: *une nuit de mai, aux rayons de la lune, sur une prairie
verdoyante, au bord d'un ruisseau limpide.* This provides the back-
drop for the transformation of arithmetic, algebra and geometry into
the three Graces through the anaphoric repetition of *toutes les trois*

and the attribution of grace, modesty, and majesty. By setting the stage in such a manner as to enable the reader to easily recognize the standard formulas of poetry, that is by appealing to a common body of experience, Lautréamont forces him to share his view of the poetry of mathematics. [29]

The apparition becomes the poet's mother, from whom he derives growth and energy:

> Vous fîtes quelques pas vers moi, avec votre longue robe flot-tante, comme une vapeur, et vous m'attirâtes vers vos fières mamelles, comme un fils béni. Alors j'accourus avec empres-sement, mes mains crispées sur votre blanche gorge. Je me suis nourri avec reconnaissance de votre manne féconde, et j'ai senti que l'humanité grandissait en moi, et devenait meilleure.
>
> (II, 10, p. 192)

The reunification of the trinity, achieved through the singular *votre longue robe* and *votre blanche gorge,* suggests that the poet views them as a totality. Furthermore, his enthusiasm is conveyed by the great number of words with flattering connotations: *vos fières mamelles, comme un fils béni, j'accourus, avec empressement, votre blanche gorge* (where the anteposition of the adjective, converging with the *style noble* of the passage, emphasizes the association of purity), *avec reconnaissance* and *votre manne féconde.* This glorifi-cation serves to reinforce the idea, in the subsequent development, that thanks to mathematics, Lautréamont has been able to remain impassive in the face of human tragedy. For, in contrast to the violent history of mankind, mathematics are imperturbable:

> Mais vous, vous restez toujours les mêmes, aucun air empesté n'effleure les rocs escarpés et les vallées immenses de votre identité.
>
> (II, 10, p. 193)

The superiority of mathematics is underlined by the pejorative connotations of *air empesté,* while the shift to an unexpected geo-logical focus, *les rocs escarpés* and *les vallées immenses,* disrupts the

---

[29] This is another instance of clichés used to create a specialized context. Cf. M. Riffaterre's comment on a concentration of clichés in Gracq's *Au Château d'Argol* : "nous n'avons pas vraiment ici la description directe d'une nature sauvage, mais bien un contexte spécialisé composé des *motifs* d'un décor roman-tique, de tout le conventionnel presque hiératique d'un opéra ; ainsi le lecteur est-il préparé à trouver un sens symbolique à ce paysage..." in "Fonctions du cliché," p. 88.

pattern set by the previous metaphoric attributions, and calls attention to itself. Now, the unpredictability, in context, of a landscape
image, converges with the reader's expectation to see, since the
Romantics, the passage of human time contrasted with the stability
of nature. And indeed, it is the permanence of mathematics which
becomes the theme:

> Vos pyramides modestes dureront davantage que les pyramides
> d'Egypte, fourmilières élevées par la stupidité de l'esclavage.
>
> (II, 10, p. 193)

The initial *pyramides,* literal in the context of geometry, are
humanized by the adjective *modestes* and serve as tenor for the comparison with the Egyptian pyramids which are animalized and
degraded by the metaphor in apposition *fourmilières élevées par la
stupidité de l'esclavage,* which personifies *stupidité.* A symbol of
human permanence becomes dehumanized while an abstract concept
(the geometric form) acquires an attribute of virtue and stability.

Mathematics will not only outlast human history, but they will
also witness the end of time:

> La fin des siècles verra encore debout sur les mines des temps,
> vos chiffres cabalistiques, vos équations laconiques et vos
> lignes sculpturales, siéger à la droite vengeresse du Tout-
> Puissant, tandis que les étoiles s'enfonceront, avec désespoir,
> comme des trombes, dans l'éternité d'une nuit horrible et uni-
> verselle, et que l'humanité grimaçante, songera à faire ses
> comptes avec le jugement dernier.
>
> (II, 10, p. 193)

The personification, in the main clause, of the end of time (*La
fin des siècles verra*) creates a concrete spectator for the survival of
the three branches of mathematics. These are referred to metony-
mically and given character epithets which endow them with mystical
and aesthetic values, and prepare the reader for their transformation
into the Son in the Holy Trinity (*siéger à la droite du Tout-Puissant*).

The first subordinate clause describes the destruction of the physical universe. The conjunction *tandis que,* which introduces it, is
frequently used to underline opposition. [30] The suggestion of height

---

[30] See Grevisse, *Le Bon Usage,* p. 862 : "*Tandis que* peut aussi marquer
la simultanéité de deux actions quelconques. On le préfère ordinairement à
pendant que quand il s'agit de deux actions contrastant l'une avec l'autre. En
outre, il s'emploie souvent dans le sens de 'au lieu de' pour marquer l'opposition..."

and stability, brought about by *encore debout, sur les ruines* and *siéger,* in the main clause, is now replaced by a suggestion of downward mobility with *les étoiles s'enfonceront, comme des trombes,* and *dans l'éternité.* This emphasizes the contrast between the permanence of mathematics and the ephemeral quality of the world.

The second subordinate clause depicts mankind insultingly (*l'humanité grimaçante*) and ironically. The abrupt shift to the colloquial *songera à faire ses comptes* breaks the apocalyptic tone of the development and thus calls attention to itself. The expression *faire ses comptes* which is normally figurative, becomes literal in the context of mathematics and consequently reminds the reader of the prosaic and commercial use that humanity makes of numbers.

The poet then thanks mathematics for having given him the weapons (i.e., prudence and logic) with which he has been able to defend himself against God and Man.

The stanza ends with a return to the religious image through the direct invocation and the epithet *saintes*:

> O mathématiques saintes, puissiez-vous, par votre commerce perpétuel, consoler le reste de mes jours de la méchanceté de l'homme et de l'injustice du Grand-Tout.

> (II, 10, p. 194)

It is significant that Lautréamont uses here *Grand-Tout* as a name for God, rather than one of his other frequently used nouns such as *le Créateur, le Tout-Puissant* or *le Céleste Bandit.* At the beginning of *Les Chants,* in the barking dogs episode, he had stated his need for infinity: "Moi, comme les chiens, j'éprouve le besoin de l'infini... je ne puis, je ne puis contenter ce besoin !" (p. 134). The ocean represents the infinite, but only figuratively: "Ta grandeur morale, image de l'infini..." (p. 141), and metaphors are means by which one may reach it: "Et, cependant, quoique je réserve une bonne part au sympathique emploi de la métaphore (cette figure de rhétorique rend beaucoup plus de services aux aspirations humaines vers l'infini que ne s'efforcent de se le figurer ceux qui sont imbus de préjugés ou d'idées fausses, ce qui est la même chose)... (p. 278). Mathematics, however, embody the concept of infinity and can make it concrete through a symbol. For Lautréamont, they are a more perfect absolute than God and satisfy better his craving for infinity. By treating them metaphorically, but without restricting himself to one figurative development he conveys to the reader the idea of the totality of mathematics. [31]

e) Metaphors which approach non-recognition.

The recognition of a metaphor depends on whether the frame and the focus share enough associated commonplaces to enable the reader to understand the analogy.   As long as the connotations of the focus remain logically consistent with the denotation of the frame, the metaphor will be understandable.   In the statement *the flow of time*, we may substitute the word *the march* or *the sands* or any other concrete word with similar associations for *the flow,* and still have a recognizable image.   But, if we substitute a word whose connotations are contrary to the idea of time progression, such as *the chair,* or whose connotations are so poor that they make figurative reading impossible, *the pencil* for instance, then the reader is forced to interpret the meaning or attempt to visualize an image which is not based on analogy.   It may, of course, be that the context provides some indication which facilitates the decoding process.

In the episode of the bees of Denderah, the now desolate temple of the Egyptian goddess of love and joy, Lautréamont compares the noise of the wings of the bees to this suffering:

> Mais si je considère la conduite de celui auquel la providence donna le trône sur cette terre, *les trois ailerons de ma douleur* font entendre un plus grand murmure.
>
> (IV, 1, p. 251)

The word *aileron* is used figuratively only in analogical transfers to other things such as *les ailerons d'un moulin à eau,* but not as a

---

[31] Lautréamont's faith in mathematics seems to have been typical of his time. Cf. G. Duby and R. Mandrou, *Histoire de la civilisation française* (Paris, 1958), II, p. 237 : "Car les triomphes scientifiques des années 1850 à 1880 sont des triomphes du mesurable, c'est-à-dire des mathématiques : trouver les instruments permettant d'observer (ou d'expérimenter) sur l'infiniment petit cellulaire, ou micro-cellulaire, l'infiniment grand (lorsque naît l'astro-physique), c'est toujours progresser sur le même chemin : la biologie fait le lien des sciences de la nature aux sciences de l'homme, et démontre la facilité d'un passage que la théorie de l'évolution, étayée des premières grandes explorations préhistoriques, soutient magistralement. Les découvertes multipliées dans le domaine des sciences naturelles ont donc suscité un enthousiasme, qui est le *fond du scientisme : la foi dans un progrès scientifique susceptible de rassembler toutes les sciences dans un seul savoir à base mathématique, qui rendrait compte de l'univers et ses galaxies, de l'homme pensant bien sûr — voire de Dieu par surplus.*" The italics are mine.

metaphorical attribution of an emotion. Yet, the bee context clarifies the comparison to some extent. However, the numerical detail *trois* remains enigmatic and prevents a clear understanding.

Lack of recognition may also be due to the fact that the focus is a word which is seldom used figuratively so that its associations depend solely on its presence in that one particular metaphor. As, when in the first stanza of Chant II, Lautréamont states that he has exposed the true nature of man:

> Dans tous les temps, il avait cru, *les paupières ployant sous les résédas de la modestie,* qu'il n'était composé que de bien et d'une quantité minime de mal.
>
> (II, 1, p. 161)

The associations of *réséda* are either of smell, as in Anatole France's *Le Réséda du curé* or of color, as in this example from Léon Bloy: "Suivant les divers états de son âme, les yeux de l'incroyable fille... s'injectaient passionnément d'écarlate, de rouge de cuivre, de points d'or, passaient ensuite au réséda de l'espérance..." [32] But, in the above case, it is *weight* that is suggested, through *ployant sous*. Since the reseda is a flower, and not a tree, the juxtaposition creates an exaggeration and the effect is ironic.

Similarly, in the following example, from the *piliers-baobabs* stanza, it is the frame which creates associations, for the focus, that are not due to its usual figurative usage:

> ... qu'il soit maudit, par ses enfants et par ma main décharnée, celui qui persiste à ne pas comprendre *les kanguroos implacables du rire et les poux audacieux de la caricature.*
>
> (IV, 2, p. 257)

I have not found any other cases where *kanguroos* is used figuratively, nor is it an animal with traditional symbolic significance, such as the snake or the wolf. Although the word has ridiculous connotations, [33] these are contradicted by the adjective *implacables* which implies seriousness and tenacity . Likewise, in the second metaphor, the pejorative connotations of *poux* are denied by the honorific *audacieux*. Without these epithets, the focus and the frame would simply

---

[32] Léon Bloy, *Le Désespéré* (Mercure de France), p. 154.
[33] Cf. Chateaubriand, *Mémoires d'Outre-Tombe*, I, XII (ed. Levaillant), p. 520: "J'allais voir à Kew les Kanguroos, ridicules bêtes, tout juste l'inverse de la girafe... quadrupèdes-sauterelles..."

create an expressive derogatory metaphor. But their presence adds ambiguity and blurs the images. However, in context, these metaphors are periphrases for Lautréamont's poetry (just before the above statement, he had written "le rire, le mal, l'orgueil, la folie, paraîtront tour à tour, entre la sensibilité et l'amour de la justice, et serviront d'exemple à la stupéfaction humaine... Il y aura, dans mes chants, une preuve imposante de puissance pour mépriser les opinions reçues. Il chante pour lui seul, et non pour ses semblables. Il ne place pas la mesure de son inspiration dans la balance humaine.") The images under discussion summarize the ambiguous character of Lautréamont's Chants: the laughter is serious and the repulsive caricatures are courageous. The metaphors' originality and mystery catch the reader's attention and convey to him the poetic purpose of the author.

2) A concrete focus in a concrete frame.

a) Clichés.

In the stanza of the *pédérastes incompréhensibles,* Maldoror has been battling with humanity:

> Le théâtre du combat n'est plus qu'un vaste champ de carnage, quand la nuit révèle sa présence et que la lune silencieuse apparaît entre *les déchirures d'un nuage.*
>
> (V, 5, p. 306)

And, in the dream episode of the *araignée de la grande espèce,* Maldoror and Elsseneur have reached a populated city:

> Les profils des dômes, les flèches des minarets et les boules de marbre des belvédères *découpaient vigoureusement leurs dentelures,* à travers les ténèbres, sur le bleu intense du ciel.
>
> (V, 7, p. 317)

In both cases, Lautréamont uses ready-made metaphors. I have found a renewed example of the first, in Zola: "Une déchirure bleue s'ouvrait derrière la nuée..."; [34] and, of the second image, in Gautier: "... les montagnes libyques découpaient sur le ciel pur leurs dentelures calcaires." [35] The example from Lautréamont is more striking, how-

---

[34] Zola, *Nana* (ed. Charpentier-Fasquelle), p. 132.
[35] Gautier, *Roman de la momie* (ed. Nelson), p. 70.

ever, because the adverb *vigoureusement* calls attention to the literal meaning of *découpaient* and rejuvenates the cliché.

In the following example, the cliché is remarkable because it serves a function in the context. It is at the very beginning of the brothel episode:

> *Une lanterne rouge, drapeau du vice,* suspendue à l'extrémité d'une tringle, balançait sa carcasse au fouet des quatre vents, au-dessus d'une porte massive et vermoulue.

> (III, 5, pp. 237-238)

The red light's identification with vice is so conventional that the use of the cliché, here, immediately sets the stage for the subsequent development. The reader recognizes it as an emblem, and this conditions his expectations.

In the next case, the cliché is renewed because the context (the ocean stanza) makes it literal:

> Ainsi, *les êtres humains, ces vagues vivantes,* meurent l'un après l'autre, d'une manière monotone ; mais sans laisser de bruit écumeux.

> (I, 9, p. 141)

In a comparison between ocean waves and human waves, the metaphor *waves of humanity* loses its figurative meaning. This is reinforced by the continuation of the analogy: *meurent l'un après l'autre, d'une manière monotone, sans laisser de bruit écumeux.*

The cliché is similarly renewed in the stanza which begins "On ne me verra pas, à mon heure dernière..." and where the poet tells how he will die:

> Que le vent, dont les sifflements plaintifs attristent l'humanité... *me porte sur les os de ses ailes,* à travers le monde, impatient de ma mort.

> (I, 10, p. 143)

Here, the commonplace metaphor *les ailes du vent* is made literal through *sur les os.* This creates a transformation of the wind into an actual bird which carries Maldoror (in the remainder of the stanza) over the world while all of Creation is watching him.

b) Original metaphors.

In the deafness stanza, the narrator describes his disillusion with the world:

> Il commençait à me sembler que *l'univers avec sa voûte étoilée de globes impassibles et agaçants,* n'était peut-être pas ce que j'avais rêvé de plus grandiose.
>
> (II, 8, p. 182)

Although *la voûte du firmament* is a common metaphor, it is used, here, as a frame for the focus *globes impassibles et agaçants.* This is striking because *globes* is downgrading in reference to stars and because the epithets *impassibles* and *agaçants* humanize *globes.* These adjectives, with their emotive connotations, express the restlessness which is the theme of the passage. [36]

In the following examples, the metaphor is used to produce a humorous effect. The first occurs in the stanza where the narrator is struck by lightning: he interprets this as a warning from God:

> *Ces agents de la police céleste* [the thunderbolts] accomplissent avec zèle leur pénible devoir, si j'en juge sommairement par mon front blessé.
>
> (II, 2, p. 164)

And in the second one, Maldoror is suspicious of an archangel, transformed into a *crabe tourteau,* who has been sent by God to save Mervyn:

> Nous verrons, à l'œuvre, s'il est aussi impérieux qu'il en a l'air; ce n'est pas un habitant de *l'abricot terrestre* ; il trahit son origine séraphique par ses yeux errants et indécis.
>
> (VI, vi, p. 347)

Without the adjective *céleste,* the first metaphor would merely convey hostility. But the epithet makes it sarcastic because in context it is both literal and figurative. It is literal, since the thunder comes from heaven, but it is also figurative, in reference to *la police.* Through the juxtaposition, its normally flattering connotations are disrupted, creating an ironic effect. In the second image, the focus *l'abricot terrestre,* because of the ridiculous connotations of *abricot,* downgrades the frame.

When the metaphoric focus dissolves the serious or sinister theme of the frame, the effect is black humor. For instance, in the shark episode:

---

[36] This image is striking enough to be listed, in the *Robert,* under the figurative uses of *voûte.*

De temps à autres je jetais les yeux vers les cités endormies sur la terre ferme ; et voyant que personne ne se doutait qu'un vaisseau allait sombrer, à quelques milles du rivage, avec *une couronne d'oiseaux de proie et un piédestal de géants aquatiques, au ventre vide,* je reprenais courage et l'espérance me revenait : j'étais donc sûr de leur perte !

(II, 13, p. 207)

La citadelle mobile [the female shark] se débarrasse facilement du dernier adversaire...

(II, 13, p. 210)

In the context of the oncoming ship-wreck, *oiseaux de proie* and *géants aquatiques, au ventre vide,* suggest the anticipation of catastrophe, but their metaphoric attributions *une couronne* and *un piédestal* destroy the ominous tone because they are mock complementary. In the second case, the alliance de mots *citadelle mobile,* which is the focus of the metaphor, produces the impression that the sinister animal is viewed ironically.

In the above metaphors, the focus weakens the normal associations of the frame and changes the character of the narration. The following images are striking because, as was the case in the concrete in abstract class, they recur as part of the themes of circularity and of torture.

Rien... si ce ne sont *les campagnes qui dansent en tourbillon* avec les arbres et les longues files d'oiseaux qui traversent les airs.

(I, 8, p. 135)

Il a dit que ce jeune homme, *broyé dans l'engrenage de mes supplices raffinés,* aurait peut-être pu devenir une intelligence de génie.

Il ouvre *les pattes anguleuses de cette hydre d'acier* [the penknife] ; et muni d'un pareil scalpel, voyant que le gazon n'avait pas encore disparu, sous la couleur de tant de sang versé, s'apprête, sans pâlir, à fouiller courageusement, le vagin de la malheureuse enfant.

(III, 2, p. 230)

The first example is in the barking dogs stanza. It is a description of what Maldoror sees when he looks out of his cavern. The personification of *les campagnes* through *qui dansent* creates a reversal of perception, a hallucination. This is reinforced by the adverbial *en tourbillon* which places the narrator at the center of the circle. The metaphor is striking because it requires the reader to adjust his perception. At the same time, it underlines the leitmotif of circularity.

Similarly, the second example, from the brothel episode, is a manifestation of the recurring theme of sado-masochism. The statement relates what Satan said to God (the speaker) about the young man (presumably the poet) he has tortured. In the metaphor, the focus, beginning with the adjective in apposition *broyé,* and continuing with *dans l'engrenage,* connotes aggressiveness, while the frame *mes supplices raffinés* suggests gratuitous sadism. But there is also an implication of masochism, because the reader has the impression that it is the poet himself who was the victim of the torture.

The third metaphor occurs in the scene where Maldoror, and his bulldog, molest a young girl. Here, the metaphor is close to a metamorphosis because the demonstrative adjective *cette* allows the frame to be replaced by the focus, whose continuation *les pattes anguleuses* completes the animalization of the knife. The image is striking, not only because of the sudden transformation of an object into a frightening animal, but also because it is thematically relevant. Bachelard points out that the penknife is functionally similar to the claw: "Il semble aussi que le canif, 'cette hydre d'acier', soit de l'ordre de l'ongle aigu. Il donne des blessures à la chair plutôt qu'aux organes. La cruauté de Lautréamont n'utilise guère le poignard dont l'action est meurtrière plutôt que cruelle." [37]

c) Non-recognition metaphors.

These examples are classified according to their degree of intelligibility: from the ones which, although unmimetic, allow the reader to determine a referent, to those which remain enigmatic after close examination. In the weakest of these images, non-recognition is due to an anomaly which can be clarified by reflection:

> Souvent, la main portée au front, debout sur les vaisseaux, tandis que *la lune se balançait entre les mâts d'une façon irrégulière,* je me suis surpris, faisant abstraction de tout ce qui n'était pas le but que je poursuivais, m'efforçant de résoudre ce difficile problème !
>
> (I, 9, pp. 138-139)

---

[37] Bachelard, pp. 36-37.

Alors son chevet est broyé par les secousses de son corps, accablé sous le poids de l'insomnie, et *il entend la sinistre respiration des rumeurs vagues de la nuit.*

(II, 15, p. 215)

In the first metaphor, from the ocean stanza, the moon, as subject of *se balançait,* acquires the motion which is proper to the ship. Since the reader can easily perceive that, from a ship-deck, the moon may appear to be moving, the enigmatic effect is not very strong. There is a similar transfer of attributes in the second example. Breathing is the characteristic of the man who is sleeping. By making *la sinistre respiration* the focus for *les rumeurs vagues de la nuit,* Lautréamont humanizes the noises and fuses all the sounds that are heard in darkness. This increases the eerie atmosphere of the situation. In both cases, the reader has to adjust his perception of reality to understand the image.

The next example is more startling, but the text itself provides an explanation. It is a description of the madwoman whose daughter has been attacked by Maldoror and his bulldog:

De longues pattes d'araignée circulent sur sa nuque ; ce ne sont autre chose que ses cheveux.

(III, 2, p. 226)

Since the metaphoric focus precedes the frame, the reader has the impression, at first, that this is a literal description. The clarification, however, indicates that the *pattes d'araignée* are figurative. This reduces the shock effect of the repulsive metamorphosis and makes the reader realize that the description is literary rather than realistic. The device, and its resulting effect, is the same as that of the similes where a mystifying vehicle is explained by the tenor.

The disruptive effect, in the following metaphors, is the result of a substitution of an unexpected term for an expected one. The first is from the hermaphrodite stanza:

Si on lui demande pourquoi il a pris la solitude pour compagne, ses yeux se lèvent vers le ciel, et retiennent avec peine une larme de reproche contre la Providence ; mais il ne répond pas à cette question imprudente, qui *répand dans la neige de ses paupières, la rougeur de la rose matinale.*

(II, 7, p. 177)

The second one is from the *l'homme à la chevelure pouilleuse* stanza:

> Je l'ai vu se diriger du côté de la mer, monter sur un promontoire déchiqueté et *battu par le sourcil de l'écume* ; et, comme une flèche, se précipiter dans les vagues.
>
> (II, 15, p. 214)

In the first case, the metaphor is created by the substitution of *la neige* for the abstract *la blancheur*. This, though, becomes clear only after the reader has seen the end of the sentence (*la rougeur de la rose matinale*). Initially, the metaphoric statement *la neige de ses paupières* is striking because the frame and the focus do not share any associations and the image appears, consequently, as surrealistic. Similarly, in the other example, *le sourcil,* which seems to be a substitution for *la crête* in the dead metaphor *la crête de l'écume,* lacks connotations that would make it consistent with the meaning of *l'écume.* This makes it difficult to interpret the statement figuratively and the image becomes a vision instead of a metaphor. In the next group of examples, the focus is so poor in connotations, that it is impossible to read the statement metaphorically. As a result, the attributions create metamorphoses rather than metaphors, transformations instead of analogies. [38]

God, in the brothel scene, tells the hair he had left behind, how the archangels discovered His debauchery:

> Mes archanges ont retrouvé, pendus *aux halliers de l'espace,* les débris flamboyants de ma tunique d'opale, qui flottaient sur les peuples béants.
>
> (III, 5, p. 244)

While Satan was watching:

> Il [Satan] a dit qu'il s'étonnait beaucoup que son orgueilleux rival, pris en flagrant délit par le succès, enfin réalisé, d'un espionnage perpétuel, pût ainsi s'abaisser jusqu'à baiser la robe de la débauche humaine, par un voyage de long cours à travers *les récifs de l'éther,* et faire périr dans les souffrances, un membre de l'humanité.
>
> (III, 5, p. 245)

---

[38] This was also the case with the more striking Homeric epithet (see Chapter III, above). From all these examples, we may deduce that, stylistically, *a metamorphosis is a metaphoric statement whose focus is so poor in associations that it must be read literally.*

Since neither *les halliers* nor *les récifs* has a realistic referent in relation to the frame, these images can only be viewed as changes in reality. Their effect is blunted because the context in which they appear is so supernatural (the narrator first sees the gigantic hair of God as a blond stick), that the reader is prepared for the unfamiliar.

That is not the situation in the next two examples, since they occur at the beginning of developments. They are more striking because they are not preceded by a pattern which conditions the reader.

The stanza of man's struggle against his conscience (II, 5) begins in this manner:

> Il y a des heures dans la vie où l'homme, à la chevelure pouil-leuse, jette, l'œil fixe, des regards fauves *sur les membranes vertes de l'espace* ; car il lui semble entendre devant lui, les ironiques huées d'un fantôme. Il chancelle et courbe la tête : ce qu'il a entendu, c'est la voix de la conscience.

> (II, 15, p. 213)

And in the stanza about the ten year old girl who follows the narrator during his daily walks, there is this self-description:

> ... celui qui ne paraissait pas s'inquiéter des maux, ni des biens de la vie présente, et s'en allait au hasard, avec une figure horriblement morte, les cheveux hérissés, la démarche chance-lante et *les bras nageant aveuglément dans les eaux ironiques de l'éther, comme pour y chercher la proie sanglante de l'espoir, ballottée continuellement, à travers les immenses régions de l'espace, par le chasse-neige implacable de la fatalité.*

> (II, 5, pp. 171-172)

Here, the statement begins with a series of features that are commonplace in descriptions of doomed Romantic heroes. But the last detail, *les bras*, sets off a metaphoric development which breaks the pattern of identifiable attributions, and mystifies the reader because its complexity makes it troublesome to understand. It is a simile with a double metaphor in both its tenor and its vehicle. In the tenor, the first focus *nageant* is continued with *les eaux ironiques* which is itself the focus of *de l'éther*. The metaphoric statement *les eaux ironiques de l'éther* is striking, as such, since it involves a sudden shift to poetic language (the plural *les eaux* and *l'éther* for air), and since the adjective *ironiques* creates an *alliance de mots* which is dif-ficult to rationalize. There is, consequently, the expectation that the vehicle will clarify the metaphor in the tenor. Yet, *comme pour y chercher* explains only *les bras nageant aveuglément*; the object of *chercher* is another metaphor which catches the reader's attention because it is a renewal of the cliché *la proie du désespoir*. [39] The qualification of *sanglante* and the substitution of *espoir* for *désespoir*, change the connotations of the frame, and the metaphor, thus, underlines the idea that, for the hero, hope is a curse. Moreover, as *ballottée continuellement* suggests, the pursuit is aimless since its object constantly drifts about. With *à travers les régions immenses de l'espace* something more striking occurs: what was viewed as the poetic use of the word *l'éther*, in the tenor, suddenly acquires a different dimension. It is generally known that the Ancients speculated that the far reaches of space were filled with ether. In the nineteenth century, ether was thought to pervade space and to serve as medium for the transmission of light waves (Faraday's assumption). Lautréamont, whose awareness of scientific theories has been proven, must have been conscious of the meaning of *l'éther* in physics. And, as I have tried to show, in reference to the plagiarized passages, he viewed scientific facts subjectively. For the reader, the two meanings of the word become fused. The discovery of the unexpected meaning is likely to prompt rereading. The image would then yield a possible interpretation: if the physical ether transmits light waves, the poetic *les eaux* is a metonymy for the scientific *les ondes,* whose own poetic usage permitted the analogy. (This is a reversal of normal poetic language, in which *les ondes* is used for water.) The implication is then that the bloody prey of hope which the narrator is seeking in darkness (*aveuglément*) is psychological light. The epithet *ironiques* could be understood as *not meaning what is says,* since *les eaux* would not be waters.

In the vehicle, the nautical connotations of *ballottée* continue the water image, but the last metaphor, *par le chasse-neige implacable de la fatalité,* shifts the focus to a wind image, at least for the reader of 1868, because the word *le chasse-neige,* in the modern sense of *snow-plow,* did not appear in the dictionary until the 1878 supplement of the *Larousse du XIXᵉ siècle.* For Lautréamont's contemporaries, *ballottée par le chasse-neige* was another fusion of water and air, as in the tenor. On account of the evolution of the linguistic code, the emphasis, for today's readers, is on *le chasse-neige implacable de la*

---

[39] Cf. Anatole France, *Le Petit Pierre* (Calmann-Lévy), p. 31: "J'étais en proie à un sombre désespoir."

fatalité since the focus and its adjective have associations which make the abstract frame dramatically concrete. [40] The change in meaning also causes *ballottée par le chasse-neige* to become an antithesis, due to the fact that the participle suggests aimless drifting and the noun connotes inexorable forward motion. This makes the ambiguity of the narrator's search for something that drifts about in space, and yet is continually kept out of reach by fate, more striking than it was initially.

I have suggested that the implied object of this search is light. The enigmatic and ambiguous way in which the idea is conveyed makes the reader participate by seeking his own light. The image would thus corroborate Blanchot's idea that Lautréamont's purpose in *Les Chants de Maldoror,* was to go from obscurity to clarity, although this is not completely achieved. [41] Furthermore, since the motion involved in the search is swimming in the air, the image verifies Bachelard's theory that Lautréamont's imagination uses the geometry of swimming and of flying to achieve its liberation. [42] Freedom and lucidity become unified.

Thematically, it seems that the identification of liberty and clarity with space, provoke the least mimetic of Lautréamont's metaphors (in the last four examples, the frame is *l'espace* or *l'éther*). The contexts in which they appear are precisely those dealing with the forces that stand in the way of freedom: conscience and God. In these situations, space, the medium through which light travels, loses its purity and becomes endowed with obstacles (*les halliers, les récifs* and *les membranes vertes*). That is because the struggle against conscience is ambivalent: although guilt stands in the way of freedom, it is also a necessity, for without awareness, there can be no freedom. The word *la conscience* means both awareness and guilt. Hence, Maldoror has to revive conscience after he has attempted to kill her, along with himself (II, 15). Blanchot comments on this passage, "Contradiction infinie: la liberté du crime exige la disparition d'un pareil témoin, mais la possibilité du crime exige sa survie." [43] The obstacles, metamorphoses, and recurrences are manifestations of the

---

[40] Cf. the English translation by Guy Wernham, *Maldoror* (New Directions, 1965) p. 62: "...his arms reaching out blindly into the ironic waters of the ether as if seeking there the bloody prey of hope, everlastingly tossed through the vast regions of space by the implacable snow-plow of fate!"

[41] Blanchot, pp. 336-337: "[Lautréamont goes] de l'implicite à l'explicite, de l'obscurité d'un secret à la claire conscience de l'obscurité, puis à la clarté de la révélation où pourtant l'obscur demeure..."

[42] Bachelard, pp. 49-50.

[43] Blanchot, p. 315.

tension which is the result of the dual nature of conscience: "... les retours, les répétitions, les identités transformées obéissent à des nécessités... et impliquent une tension toujours plus forte entre ce qui est clair et ce qui ne veut pas le devenir, entre la lucidité toute-puissante du dehors et la perfide lucidité du dedans qui, prisonnière d'elle-même, est aussi complice de sa prison." [44]

In both classes of metaphors, the most salient examples remain enigmatic. Because of this, the reader must visualize and interpret them. The metaphors which are immediately comprehensible, even when they are highly original, demand less involvement because they provide all the information. But the metaphors which I have classified as non-recognition types require an active participation in the act of creation, since the reader has to account for what is left out and mysterious. The interpretation which is then provided need not be the only one possible. The important aspect, from an affective point of view, is that the reader has to become involved in the poem. "Le poète est celui qui inspire bien plus que celui qui est inspiré," wrote Eluard "Les poèmes ont toujours de grandes marges blanches où la mémoire ardente se consume pour recréer un délire sans passé. Leur principale qualité est non pas, je le répète, d'invoquer, mais d'inspirer.... La compréhension, comme le désir, comme la haine, est faite entre la chose à comprendre et les autres, comprises ou incomprises." [45]

---

[44] *Op. cit.*, p. 300.
[45] *Donner à voir*, p. 81.

CONCLUSION

The aim of stylistic analysis is to objectively locate and describe expressive and affective devices. After this has been accomplished, it becomes possible to attempt an evaluation, to proceed from stylistics to literary interpretation.

In the methods of Leo Spitzer and of Erich Auerbach, the linguistic feature was shown to be indicative of the psychological, historical or sociological context of the author or of the period in which the work was written. The weakness of the procedure, besides being too dependent on the erudition of one scholar, is that it connects style to literary history rather than to literary criticism.

This conclusion will try to integrate the stylistic analysis of Lautréamont's imagery with other modes of investigation (the essentially psychoanalytic reading of Pleynet and the myth reading of Zweig) and to arrive thereby, it is hoped, at a more complete understanding of the work. In this manner stylistics would serve to corroborate, correct or dispute, not the validity of these other readings, but their evaluations. Impressionism will be minimized because different exegeses will have been verified by a methodical textual scrutiny. And, since throughout my study, the emphasis has been on the shock effect of the imagery, the converging judgments might enable us to determine why, when we read Lautréamont, "les cadres de l'esprit semblent à jamais pulvérisés." [1]

The reader brings to the texts certain expectations which are the result of his culture. Since these expectations are being constantly denied, it is his culture that is being put into question. He opens the book and, because of literary experience, anticipates a *story* with a linear development—a beginning, a middle and an end—where things happen as a consequence of one another. But there is no story, no object that the subject is about. This can only mean that the subject matter is nothing but itself, which, as Marcelin Pleynet emphasizes,

---

[1] Léon Pierre-Quint, *Le Comte de Lautréamont et Dieu*, p. 173.

must be the reader. [2] Not only does Lautréamont say it at the very beginning ("Plût au ciel que le lecteur, enhardi et devenu momentanément féroce comme ce qu'il lit, trouve, sans se désorienter, son chemin abrupt et sauvage, à travers les pages sombres et pleines de poison...", p. 123), but the non-linear development involves the reader directly.   In a linear progression, the stanzas would be in sequence, one starting where the last one ended.   In *Les Chants,* the stanzas seem to have no relationship to each other.   This means that every stanza is a new beginning, stands in isolation, and is part of a mosaic, as in Rimbaud's *Les Illuminations.* [3]   The development is elliptical and Lautréamont tells us so in Chant V.   In an ellipsis, the reader must supply his own connections and is thereby forced to participate. [4]

Since it is the reader who is at issue with the first few words, we must begin by establishing what the reader's own *story* would be. Here, we can only follow Pleynet and say that it is "mythe-rhétorique-inconscient." [5]

From the point of view of the unconscious, Freud is no help as long as he is being used to interpret an author, an individual who

---

[2] "Dès la première ligne, dès la première strophe du premier chant, nous n'entrons pas ailleurs que dans cet espace de la lecture, nous ne rencontrons pas d'autre fiction que celle que nous posons, que nous constituons comme lecteur (comme "le lecteur"), pas d'autres limites que les nôtres: dans la mesure où nous pouvons devenir *comme* ce que nous lisons, dans la mesure où nous pouvons nous trouver désorientés où nous apporterons et n'apporterons pas une *logique rigoureuse et une tension d'esprit égale au moins à notre défiance.*" *Lautréamont par lui-même*, p. 109.

[3] Angus Fletcher, *Allegory*, points out that surrealist isolation of parts, is a traditional allegorical device: " An allegorical world gives us objects all lined up, as it were, on the frontal plane of a mosaic, each with its own 'true', unchanging size and shape... Religious painting demonstrates this isolation in showing descents of angels who visit mankind in completely discrete, discontinuous forms. Even more isolation is apparent when we turn to the diabolical imagery that accompanies the histories of saints or pictures of the Day of Judgment. So too the imagery of modern surrealism, metonymic and synecdochic in character, presents the *objet trouvé*, which has a direct antecedent in the emblematic devices of the earlier centuries. These latter devices are likewise 'found objects,' although they are organized into traditional iconographies which we recognize more readily than the chiefly Freudian iconography of surrealism." pp. 104-106.

[4] Fletcher, *ibid.*, p. 107, "The price of a lack of mimetic naturalness is what the allegorist, like the Metaphysical, poet, must pay in order to force his reader into an analytic frame of mind. Ellipsis in speech has just this effect, in much the same way that any fragmentary utterance (the rhetorician's *aposiopesis*) takes on the appearance of a coded message needing to be deciphered. We shall find that a strict order of elements is another aspect of the allegorical coding process, but for the moment it suffices to point out that by having a surrealistic surface texture allegory immediately elicits an interpretive response from the reader."

[5] Pleynet, *op. cit.*, p. 128.

doesn't exist: Lautréamont is only a creation of Isidore Ducasse, who did his best to erase his identity. (The first edition of the first Chant was even published without any author's name, and the one biographical reference—Georges Dazet—disappears in subsequent editions). [6] The author is the reader himself and Lautréamont only in so far as he is his own reader. The mistake of a Freudian interpretation such as Marcel Jean and Arpad Mezei's *Maldoror* is that it considers the text as the expression of the experience of an individual, as probably Freud himself would have done, instead of the neurosis of a culture. When Freud turned his attention to culture, in *Civilization and Its Discontents,* his evaluation was that repression of the instincts was a condition for the survival of civilization, hence that the status quo, which is life governed by the reality principle, is the only possible life. An unrepressed civilization, i.e. life governed by the pleasure principle, of which imagination is the surviving manifestation, would be impossible. This conclusion explains Freud's incomprehension of what the surrealists were trying to accomplish. [7]

The reader's expectations are the products of a culture dominated by the reality principle: logic, lineality, cause and effect, clearly defined categories, etc. The book, by denying the expectations, negates these repressions and becomes an assertion of the pleasure principle, of the life instinct. Freud is therefore relevant only if we disregard his value judgment and consider the possibility of an unrepressed life. In recent years, there have been several studies which envisage this reinterpretation: Herbert Marcuse's *Eros and Civilization: A Philosophical Inquiry into Freud* (Boston, 1955), and Norman O. Brown's *Life Against Death* (New York, 1959) and *Love's Body* (New York, 1966). In the light of these essays, it becomes clear that Lautréamont's experience, and ours as we read him, is the result of the basic reversal of reality-pleasure principles, that all the reversals in the book are the logical consequence of that initial step.

On the archetypal level of mythology the culture heroes of repressive civilization are Prometheus who "is the trickster and (suffering) rebel against the gods, who creates culture at the price of perpetual pain. He symbolizes productiveness, the unceasing effort to master life; but in his productivity, blessing and curse, progress and toil are

---

[6] Pleynet, pp. 113 and 129. For Georges Dazet, see above (p. 59 n. 12).
[7] See in this connection, André Breton "Interview du Professeur Freud" in *Les Pas perdus,* pp. 117-118, and the Breton-Freud correspondance in *Le Surréalisme au service de la révolution,* vol. V, p. 11.

inextricably intertwined," [8] and Apollo: "Apollo is the god of form—
of plastic form in art, of rational form in thought, of civilized form
in life. But the Apollonian form is form as the negation of instinct." [9]
Yet, mythology also has heroes who represent the taboo side of the
culture : Orpheus, Narcissus and Dionysus. "The Orphic and Narcis-
sitic experience of the world negates that which sustains the world
of the performance principle. The opposition between man and
nature, subject and object, is overcome." [10] Paul Zweig has analyzed
the Narcissus aspect of Lautréamont's attempt and revealed that its
major manifestation is found in the circularity of the themes and of
the composition. [11]

The Orphic element is apparent in the very title *Les Chants de*
Maldoror, in the homosexual episodes and in the stated purpose of
going back to the beginning of poetry: "La science que j'entreprends
est une science distincte de la poésie. Je ne chante pas cette dernière.
Je m'efforce de découvrir sa source." (p. 388). And Maldoror has the
aspect of Dionysus when he appears as "the antagonist of the god
who sanctions logic, the realm of reason" [12] and as the hermaphodite
(II, 7) because "Instead of negating, he [Dionysus] affirms the dialectical unity of the great instinctual opposites: Dionysus reunifies
male and female, Self and Other, life and death. Dionysus is the
image of the instinctual reality which psychoanalysis will find the
other side of the veil." [13] Significant also in this context is the Ocean
stanza: Marcuse says that "Freud describes the 'ideational context'
of the surviving primary ego-feeling as 'limitless extension and one-
ness with the universe' (oceanic feeling). And later in the same chapter
he suggests that the oceanic feeling seeks to reinstate 'limitless nar-
cissisms.' " [14]

On the level of rhetoric, imagery provides a perfect frame-work
in this search for the limitless, and Lautréamont knew it: "... la métaphore (cette figure de rhétorique rend beaucoup plus de services aux
aspirations humaines vers l'infini que ne s'efforcent de se le figurer
ceux qui sont imbus de préjugés ou d'idées fausses, ce qui est la
même chose)..." (p. 278). In a simile, we have two literal sets of

---

[8] Marcuse, *Eros and Civilization* (Vintage Books), p. 146.
[9] Brown, *Life Against Death*, p. 174.
[10] Marcuse, *op cit.*, pp. 150-151.
[11] Paul Zweig, "Lautréamont ou les violences du Narcisse," p. 11.
[12] Marcuse, p. 146.
[13] Brown *op cit.*, p. 175.
[14] Marcuse, p. 153.

meaning, the tenor which belongs to the fiction and the vehicle which is provided by the poet's imagination and thus brings in material that is foreign to the fiction. The simile, as a unit, brings together these two realities and creates an image by establishing a correspondence between them. The content of the vehicle is selected arbitrarily for what is considered traditionally as a functional or ornamental purpose. In Lautréamont's similes, we are constantly reminded that it is the fiction itself, the tenor, which is arbitrary, i.e. the product of the imagination, while it is the vehicle which brings in reality. Hence, the numerous literary sources, other fictions, are used as tenor for the plagiarized, but true, scientific material of the vehicle (and Lautréamont's plagiarisms are always in the vehicle) as well as for the fantasy material, since fantasy is imagination not dominated by the reality principle and, consequently, also true. This reversal calls into question the arbitrariness of all fictions: it is just as arbitrary to find a sunset beautiful as it is to find the fortuitous encounter beautiful. [15] The tenor is then an arbitrarily selected point, at which the poet is standing, and from which he can elliptically encompass the world around him. This is the technique which Lautréamont himself reveals at the beginning of Chant III: "Amour affamé de la race humaine, qui se dévorerait lui-même, s'il ne cherchait sa nourriture dans les fictions célestes: créant, à la longue, une pyramide de séraphins, plus nombreux que les insectes qui fourmillent dans une goutte d'eau, il les entrelacera dans une ellipse qu'il fera tourbillonner autour de lui." (p. 220). [16]

In metaphors, there is a figurative focus in a literal frame. The literal meaning of a word is the dictionary meaning, the realistic usage. The figurative meaning of a word is the imaginative usage. In a traditional metaphor, the focus is restricted by the frame because the words must share some associated commonplaces for their interaction to be logical. In other words, the focus has to have enough connotations so that the reader may recognize that it is used metaphorically. Imagination is dominated by the reality principle, by the finite. If, however, as is the case in Lautréamont's more salient examples, the focus is too poor in associations to be read figuratively (*les halliers de l'espace*), then there is a fusion of reality and imagination,

---

[15] See Pleynet, "Le Topos du monde renversé," in *Lautréamont par lui-même*, pp. 136-137.
[16] Pleynet quotes Emile Benveniste who suggests that the ellipsis is the proper device for symbolic connections, *op. cit.*, pp. 130-131.

a metamorphosis. But this is only possible when both the focus and the frame are concrete. When the focus is in an abstract frame (*les kanguroos implacables du rire et les poux audacieux de la caricature*) it cannot be viewed as a physical transformation of the world and becomes a nonsense metaphor, which means that it is free from the finiteness imposed upon it by reality, and not forced into the recognizable category of imagination. This unsettles the reader who is accustomed to clearly be able to see the figurative word and the literal word, to be able to distinguish between reality and imagination.

Paradoxically, the fusion of categories involves a fragmentation of our normal perception, real unity is actually fraction. Paul Zweig thinks that, because of the metamorphoses of Chants IV and V, Lautréamont's Narcissistic experience is ultimately a failure: "Lautréamont a fait de son poème un 'tourbillon' dont il devait être lui-même le centre. Il a voulu étendre le règne de ses images pour que chaque moment du cercle reflète son désir de Narcisse. Mais à la fin la violence bouleverse l'univers de ses fictions.... Les métamorphoses expriment l'écartèlement de cette vision d'un Narcisse qui a voulu trouver son image au sein d'un océan de formes fracassées. Car l'image qu'il y découvre a subi aussi la magie des renversements. L'échec paradoxal de Narcisse lui a rendu sa propre forme méconnaissable." [17]

This conclusion is reached because of the basic assumption that the narcissism in *Les Chants* is the manifestation of an individual personality, that the metamorphoses shatter an ego which had attempted to make the world like itself. However, Isidore Ducasse, by making the author of *Les Chants* a known fictional character (Eugène Sue's Latréaumont [sic]) [18] and by erasing from this work all biographical references, depersonalized himself. The narcissism in *Les Chants* is therefore *primary narcissism,* the feeling which exists before the differentiation of the Self and the Other. "It is significant that the introduction of narcissism into psychoanalysis," writes Marcuse, "marked a turning point in the development of the instinct theory: the assumption of independent ego instincts (the self-preservation instincts) was shaken and replaced by the notion of an undifferentiated, unified libido prior to the division into ego and external objects." [19] The metamorphoses in *Les Chants,* instead of destroying the ego, are steps toward the creation of the person. Lautréamont becomes the

[17] Zweig, loc. cit., p. 63.
[18] On Sue's *Latréaumont,* see Jean and Mezei, *Maldoror,* pp. 167-177.
[19] Marcuse, p. 152.

creator of Isidore Ducasse, i.e. his own father: "... le pseudonyme (Lautréamont) a permis au nom propre d'avoir un autre référent que l'héritage paternel (le référent évident du nom propre). Ducasse est désormais le fils de ses œuvres." [20] He could thus have said, like Artaud, "Moi, Antonin Artaud, je suis mon fils / mon père, ma mère / et moi." [21]

The beginning of the book is for Ducasse, as well as for the reader, a return to the Beginning, that is to a prebiographical and pre-historical situation. Biography and history begin with *Poésies*. For, while in *Les Chants* every effort was made to erase personal references, *Poésies* lists not only Isidore Ducasse as author but dedicatees whose relationship to the author is clearly indicated ("A mes condisciples", "Aux Directeurs de Revues", "A Monsieur Hinstin, mon ancien professeur de rhétorique"). It is revealing that it is through the names which appear in this dedication that most of the biographical research on Lautréamont has been accomplished. And, while the characters that are used in *Les Chants* suggest typically fictitious heroes (Maldoror, Falmer, Lohengrin, Lombano, Léman, Mervyn, etc.), *Poésies* refers to literary figures, to the cultural history of Ducasse and of his reader. What is really shattered in *Les Chants* is not the identity of Narcissus, but the lack of identity—Lautréamont and Maldoror. After the fragmentation, there is the personality of the author of *Poésies*.

These are not a reversal, a return to orthodoxy. They are, rather, a logical outcome of the initial reversal which placed the work on the side of the taboo. They do not represent a reassertion of goodness, in a dialectical struggle between good and evil, but the destruction of the dialectical situation. As Philippe Sollers remarks, "L'englobement va substituer à l'*ambiguïté* contradictoire de l'époque parlante un redoublement, une répétition destinés à marquer le milieu de la séparation sans communication de l'affirmation et de la négation: non plus la loi d'une unité confuse et double (passant de l'un à l'autre sans savoir dire ni oui ni non) mais les lois d'un *ordre* duel de permutation (où tout est oui/tout est non)." [22] The form which is best suited for this "ordre duel de permutation" is the aphorism, the form

---

[20] Pleynet, *op. cit.*, p. 157.
[21] Quoted by Philippe Sollers, "La Science de Lautréamont," *Critique*, 245 (October 1967), 794, n. 3.
[22] Sollers, *ibid.*, p. 824.

of *Poésies*. An aphorism is a fragmented form which gives everything at once, without any need for justification: "La maxime n'a pas besoin d'elle [la vérité] pour se prouver. Un raisonnement demande un raisonnement. La maxime est une loi qui sentence un ensemble de raisonnements. Un raisonnement se complète à mesure qu'il s'appro-che de la maxime. Devenu maxime, sa perfection rejette les preuves de la métamorphose" (p. 380). Hence, the clear awareness of the arbitrariness of fictions, of "tics", of descriptions: "Les descriptions sont une prairie, trois rhinocéros, la moitié d'un catafalque. Elles peuvent être le souvenir, la prophétie. Elles ne sont pas le para-graphe que je viens de terminer" (pp. 383-384). No matter what its content may be, an aphorism is always true: Pascal, La Rochefou-cauld, Vauvenargues can be corrected in the sense of optimism, but the form remains. They become Ducasse corrected in the sense of pessimism. Stated as an aphorism, an idea is no longer subject to critical scrutiny: "Il faut que la critique attaque la forme, jamais le fond de vos idées, de vos phrases. Arrangez-vous." (p. 374). This is what Camus, when he spoke of "les banalités laborieuses des *Poésies*," [23] did not seem to realize. Commencement addresses may contain nothing but banalities. Yet it is certainly not banal *to say* that "Les chefs-d'œuvre de la langue française sont les discours de distribution pour les lycées, et les discours académiques" (p. 364). As the title of the work indicates, these statements are to be regarded, not as *Pensées* or *Sentences* or *Maximes,* but as *Poésies.* It was Lautréamont's discovery that the fragmented form of the aphorism is the poetic form which unifies opposites, which is capable of satis-fying his *besoin d'infini.* In the words of Norman O. Brown, "Aphorism is exaggeration or grotesque; in psychoanalysis nothing is true except the exaggerations; and in poetry 'cet extrémisme est le phénomène même de l'élan poétique.' Aphorism is exaggeration, extravagant language; the road of excess which leads to the palace of wisdom.... Aphorism, the form of the mad truth, the Dionysian form." [24]

The remarkable aspect of Lautréamont's work is the consistency with which it is developed, from the initial reversal of author as reader and reader as author, that is from the moment it became narcissistic and replaced the reality principle with the pleasure prin-

[23] Albert Camus, *L'Homme révolté* (Gallimard, 1951), p. 105.
[24] Brown, *Love's Body*, p. 187. Quote from Bachelard, *La Poétique de l'espace*, p. 189.

ciple. I do not mean to imply that Lautréamont knew what the outcome of the experience would be. He did not know that any more than the reader. But he realized from the very first stanza that the Apollonian cultural norms of the reader would be destroyed. That is why he advised him to act like the crane who is not stupid and to take "un autre chemin philosophique et plus sûr."

———

BIBLIOGRAPHY

This bibliography restricts itself to works on Lautréamont which have influenced the present study. But it does bring up to date Hector Talvart and Joseph Place's *Bibliographie des auteurs modernes de langue française,* tome onzième, Paris: Horizons de France (1952), pp. 340-348, and Pierre Capretz' "Eléments d'une bibliographie ducassienne" in *Œuvres complètes,* Paris: Corti (1958), pp. 405-420. Since both of these bibliographies have complete descriptions of the various editions, I mention only those recent editions which are most helpful for research. The reader may also consult Miroslav Karaulac's "Esquisse d'une bibliographie sur Lautréamont," *Bulletin des Jeunes Romanistes,* 1 (1960), 27-32.

For methods of imagery analysis, I list the works on which my approach is based and some of the most fundamental studies in stylistics. More complete information can be found in Helmut A. Hatzfeld, *A Critical Bibliography of the New Stylistics Applied to the Romance Literatures,* 1900-1952, 1953-1965, Chapel Hill: The University of North Carolina Press (1953, 1966), and in Hatzfeld and Le Hir, *Essai de bibliographie critique de stylistique française et romane,* 1955-1960, Université de Grenoble (1961).

Also included in this bibliography are works of cultural criticism which I have used for purposes of evaluation.

1. *Editions of Lautréamont.*

Œuvres complètes. Introduction by André Breton. Paris: G. L. M., 1938.

Œuvres complètes. Introduction by L. Genonceaux, R. de Gourmont, Ed. Jaloux, A. Breton, Ph. Soupault, J. Gracq, R. Caillois, H. Blanchot. Paris: José Corti, 1953.

Œuvres complètes. Same as above but with bibliography by Pierre Capretz. Paris: José Corti, 1958, 1963.

Œuvres complètes. With "Notes pour une vie d'Isidore Ducasse et de ses écrits" by Maurice Saillet. Paris: Le Livre de Poche, 1963.

Les Chants de Maldoror. With "Crimes du langage" by Hubert Juin. Paris: Club Géant, 1967.

Poésies. First commented edition, by Georges Goldfayn and Gérard Legrand. Paris: Le Terrain vague, 1960.

Maldoror. English translation by Guy Wernham. Mount Vernon: Golden Eagle Press, 1943.

Maldoror. Including *Poésies*. Same as above, but with Introduction by James Laughlin. New York: New Directions, 1965.

2. *Works on Lautréamont, stylistics, literary criticism, etc.*

Alicot, François. "Lautréamont. A propos des chants de Maldoror, "*Mercure de France*, January 1, 1928, pp. 199-206.

Alquié, Ferdinand. *Philosophie du surréalisme*. Paris: Flammarion, 1955.

Antoine, Gerald. "Pour une méthode d'analyse stylistique des images," *AHC*, Paris: Les Belles Lettres, 1961.

Aragon, Louis. "Contribution à l'avortement des études maldororiennes," *Le Surréalisme au service de la révolution*, no. 2 (1921), 22-24.

Aragon, Louis. "Préface à Maldoror, Lautréamont," *Ecrits Nouveaux*, August-September 1922.

Aragon, Louis, André Breton and Paul Eluard. *Lautréamont envers et contre tout*. Paris: Ed. Surréalistes, 1927.

Aragon, Louis. *Le Traité du style*. Paris: Gallimard, 1928.

Arc (L'). Special issue on Lautréamont, no. 33, octobre-novembre, 1967.

Auerbach, Eric. *Mimesis*. New York: Anchor Books, 1957.

Bachelard, Gaston. *Lautréamont*. Paris: José Corti, 1939, 1963.

Balakian, Anna. *Literary Origins of Surrealism*. New York: King's Crown Press, 1947.

Balakian, Anna. "The Surrealist Image," *RR*, 44 (1953), 273-281.

Balakian, Anna. *Surrealism: The Road to the Absolute*. New York: Noonday Press, 1959.

Balakian, Anna. "*Metaphors and Metamorphosis in André Breton's Poetics*," *FS*, 19 (1965), 34-41.

Barthes, Roland. *Le Degré zéro de l'écriture*. Paris: Seuil, 1953.

Beardsley, Monroe C. *Aesthetics: Problems in the Philosophy of Criticism*. New York: The Macmillan Company, 1958.

Bernard, Suzanne. *Le Poème en prose de Baudelaire jusqu'à nos jours*. Paris: Nizet, 1959.

Black, Max. *Models and Metaphors*. Ithaca: Cornell University Press, 1962.

Blanchot, Maurice. "Lautréamont et le mirage des sources," *Critique*, XXV (June 1948), 483-498.

Blanchot, Maurice. *Lautréamont et Sade*. Paris: Ed. de Minuit, 1949, 1963.

Bonnet, Henri. *Roman et poésie*. Paris: Nizet, 1951.

Bonnet, Marguerite. "Lautréamont et Michelet," *RHL*, LXIV (1964), 605-622.

Breton, André. *Manifestes du surréalisme*. Paris: coll. Idées, Gallimard, 1963.

Breton, André. *Les Pas perdus*. Paris: Gallimard, 1924.

Breton, André. "Isidore Ducasse," *Littérature*, December 1929.

Breton, André. *Anthologie de l'humour noir*. Paris: Ed. du Sagittaire, 1940.

Breton, André, "Sucre jaune — A propos de Lautréamont André Breton répond à Albert Camus," *Arts*, no. 328 (October 12, 1951), 1.

Breton, André. *Entretiens.* Paris: Gallimard, 1952.

Bütler, Sonja. *Untersuchungen uber den französischen Prosarhythmus an Texten von Lautréamont.* Zurich: Diss. Phil., 1956.

Brooke-Rose, Christine. *A Grammar of Metaphor.* London: Secher and Warburg, 1958.

Brooks, Cleanth. *The Well Wrought Urn.* New York: Harvest Books, 1947.

Brown, Norman O. *Life Against Death.* New York: Vintage Books, 1959.

Brown, Norman O. *Love's Body.* New York: Randon House, 1966.

Caillois, Roger. "Après Rimbaud et Lautréamont," *Cahiers de la Pléiade,* April 1947, pp. 141-145.

Caillois, Roger. "La Littérature de révolte," *Revue de Paris,* April 1940, pp. 125-131.

Camus, Albert. *L'homme révolté.* Paris: Gallimard, 1951.

Carrouges, Michel. *La Mystique du surhomme.* Paris: Gallimard, 1949.

Carmody, Francis J. "Le Diable des bestiaires," *CAIEF,* 3-4-5 (1953), 79-85.

Carmody, Francis. "A Correlation of the Chronology and Lexicon of Rimbauds's Verse," *FR,* XXXIII (1960), 247-256.

Castex, Pierre-Georges. *Le Conte fantastique en France de Nodier à Maupassant.* Paris: José Corti, 1951.

Cressot, Marcel. *Le Style et ses techniques.* Paris: Presses Univ. de France, 1951.

Daniélou, Jean. *Platonisme et théologie mystique.* Paris: Aubier, Ed. Montaigne, 1944.

Disque vert. "Le Cas Lautréamont," Paris-Bruxelles, 1925.

Eigeldinger, Marc. *L'Evolution dynamique de l'image au dix-neuvième siècle.* Neuchâtel: La Baconnière, 1943.

Eliade, Mircea. *Le Mythe de l'éternel retour.* Paris: Gallimard, 1949.

Eluard, Paul. "Vauvenargues et Lautréamont," *Minotaure,* no. X, 1937.

Eluard, Paul. *Donner à voir.* Paris: Gallimard, 1939.

Engler, Winfried. "Die Metamorphosen in den *Chants de Maldoror* von Lautréamont," *Antaios,* III (March 1962), 560-572.

Fletcher, Angus. *Allegory.* Ithaca: Cornell University Press, 1964.

Fowler, Roger, ed. *Essays on Style and Language.* London: Routledge and Kegan Paul, 1966.

Fowlie, Wallace. *Age of Surrealism.* Bloomington: Indiana University Press, 1960.

Friesman, Norman. "Imagery: From Sensation to Symbol," *JAe,* 12 (1953), 25-37.

Gourmont, Remy de. "La Littérature. Maldoror," *Mercure de France,* February 1891, pp. 97-106.

Gourmont, Remy de. *Le Livre de masques.* Paris: Mercure de France, 1896.

Graaf, Daniel A. de. "Du nouveau sur la mort de Lautréamont," *Neophil,* XLII (1958), 182-186.

Graaf, Daniel A. de. "Het leven van Lautréamont," *VLG,* XLVII (1963), 477-488.

Greene, Thomas. "The Relevance of Lautréamont," *Partisan Review,* XXI (Sept.-Oct. 1954), 528-539.

Greenfield, Stanley B. "Grammar and Meaning in Poetry," *PMLA*, 5 (1967), 377-387.

Grubbs, H. A. "The Problem of Lautréamont," *RR*, 25 (1934), 140-150.

Grubbs, H. A. "The Pseudonym of Isidore Ducasse," *MLN*, LXVI (1951), 98-102.

Grubbs, H. A. "The Division into Strophes of the *Chants de Maldoror,*" *HLN*, LXVIII (1953), 154-157.

Guillot-Munoz, Alvaro and Gerasio Guillot-Munoz. *Lautréamont et Laforgue.* Montevideo: Agencia General de Libreria y Publicaciones, 1925.

Guiraud, Pierre. *La Stylistique.* Paris: coll. "Que sais-je?" Presses Universitaires de France, 1954.

Guyard, Marius-François. "Lautréamont et Lamartine." *TLL*, 111 (1965), ii, 77-82.

Haac, Oscar. "Lautréamont's Conversions: The Structure and Meaning of *Poésies,*" MLN, LXV (1950), 369-375.

Henle, Paul. *Language, Thought and Culture.* Ann Arbor: Michigan University Press, 1958.

Hornstein, L. N. "Analysis of Imagery: A Critique of Literary Method." *PMLA*, LVII (1942), 638-655.

Huguet, Edmond. *Les Comparaisons et les métaphores de Victor Hugo.* Paris: Hachette, 1904.

Hytier, Jean. *Le Plaisir poétique.* Paris: Presses Universitaires de France, 1923.

Hytier, Jean. *Les Arts de littérature.* Paris: Charlot, 1945.

Ivsic, Radovan. "Le Plagiat des coquilles n'est pas nécessaire," *La Brèche,* 6 (June 1964), 59-66.

Ivsic, Radovan. "A Quand?" *La Brèche,* 7 (Dec. 1964), 106-107.

Jean, Marcel and Arpad Mezei. *Maldoror.* Paris: Ed. du Pavois, 1947.

Jean, Marcel. *Genèse de la pensée moderne.* Paris: Corrêa, 1950.

Kalow, Gert. "Lautréamont: Utopie der burgerlichen Moral," *Zwischen Christentum und Ideologie.* Heidelberg: W. Rothe, 1956, pp. 23-60.

Konrad, Hedwig. *Etude sur la métaphore.* Paris: Lavergne, 1939.

Kristeva, Julia. "Pour une sémiologie des paragrammes," *Tel Quel*, 29 (1967), 53-75.

Larbaud, Valery. *Lautréamont.* Liège: Editions Dynamo, 1957.

Lewis, C. Day. *The Poetic Image.* London: Cape, 1947.

Lobet, Marcel. "D'une littérature démoniaque ou prométhéenne," *Revue Générale Belge,* 11 (Nov. 1966), 21-35.

Lodge, David. *Language of Fiction.* New York: Columbia University Press, 1966.

Malraux, André. "La Genèse des chants de Maldoror," *Action* (April 1920), pp. 33-35.

Marcenac, Jean. "Lautréamont et la logique de la poésie," *La Nouvelle Critique,* 154 (April 1964), 7-49.

Marcuse, Herbert. *Eros and Civilization: A Philosophical Inquiry into Freud.* Boston: Beacon Press, 1955.

Marouzeau, Jules. *Précis de stylistique française.* Paris: Masson, 1946.

Morier, Henry. *Dictionnaire de poétique et de rhétorique.* Paris: Presses Universitaires de France, 1961.

Mourot, Jean. "Stylistique des intentions et stylistique des effets," *CAIEF,* 16 (1964), 71-79.

Nadeau, Maurice. *Histoire du surréalisme.* Paris: Seuil, 1947.

Nadeau, Maurice. *Documents surréalistes.* Paris: Seuil, 1948.

Nowottny, Winifred. *The Language Poets Use.* London: Oxford University Press, 1962.

O'Brien, Justin. "A Rapprochement: M. André Gide and Lautréamont," *RR,* Feb. 1937, pp. 54-58.

Patri, Aimé. "Fantomas en mal d'Aurore," *Preuves,* 166 (1964), 76-82.

Pia, Pascal. "Schizophrène, ou pince-sans-rire," *Carrefour* 1058 (Jan. 6, 1965), 18.

Planté, Louis. *Isidore Ducasse comte de Lautréamont d'après un dossier tarbais.* Edit. Pyrénéennes, 1966.

Ponge, Francis. "Le Dispositif Maldoror — poésies," *Le Grand Recueil,* II, pp. 203-205, Paris: Gallimard, 1961.

Pleynet, Marcelin. "Les Chants de Maldoror et de Lautréamont," *Tel Quel* 26 (1966), 42-59.

Pleynet, Marcelin. *Lautréamont par lui-même.* Paris: Seuil, 1967.

Pongs, Hermann. *Das Bild in der Dichtung.* 2 vols. Marburg, 1960, 1963.

Richards, I. A. *The Philosophy of Rhetoric.* New York: Oxford University Press, 1936.

Riffaterre, Michael. *Le Style des Pléiades de Gobineau.* New York: Columbia University Press, 1957.

Riffaterre, Michael. "Criteria for Style Analysis," *Word,* XV (1959), 154-174.

Riffaterre, Michael. "Stylistic Context," *Word,* XVI (1960), 207-218.

Riffaterre, Michael. "Vers la définition linguistique du style," *Word,* XVII (1961), 328-344.

Riffaterre, Michael. "Problèmes d'analyse du style littéraire," *Romance Philology,* XIV (1961), 216-227.

Riffaterre, Michael. "Comment décrire le style de Chateaubriand," *RR,* LIII (1962), 128-138.

Riffaterre, Michael. "La Vision hallucinatoire chez Victor Hugo," *MLN,* 78 (1963), 225-141.

Riffaterre, Michael. "Fonctions du cliché dans la prose littéraire," *CAIEF,* 16 (1964), 81-95.

Riffaterre, Michael. "L'Etude stylistique des formes littéraires conventionnelles," *FR,* 38 (1964), 3-14.

Riffatterre, Michael, "Describing Poetic Structures: Two Approaches to Baudelaire's *Les Chats,*" *YFS,* 36-37 (1966), 200-242.

Rispal, Yvonne. "Le Monde de Lautréamont à travers l'étude du langage," *Cahiers du Groupe Françoise Minkowska* (Paris), October 1962, pp. 8-50.

Rochon, Lucienne. "Le Professeur de rhétorique de Lautréamont: Gustave Hinstin," *Europe,* 449 (September 1966), 153-189.

Rouzet, Georges. "Au Livre de Poche, les Chants de Maldoror," *La Revue Nationale,* 368 (Oct. 1964), 277-278.

Saillet, Maurice. "Défense du plagiat," *LetN,* 2 (April 1953), 205-214.

Saillet, Maurice. "Les Inventeurs de Maldoror," *LetN,* 14, 15, 16, 17 (April to July 1954).
Sayce, Richard A. *Style in French Prose.* Oxford: Clarendon Press, 1953.
Schaefer, Dietrich. "Lautréamont: Das Gesamtwerk," *Neue Deutsche Hefte,* 99 (May-June 1964), 118-122.
Sebeok, T. A., ed. *Style in Language.* Cambridge: M.I.T. Press, 1959.
Sollers, Philippe. "La Science de Lautréamont," *Critique,* 245 (October 1967), 791-833.
Soulier, Jean-Pierre. *Lautréamont, génie ou maladie mentale?* Genève: Droz, 1964.
Soupault, Philippe. *Lautréamont.* Paris: Seghers, 1946.
Spitzer, Leo. *Stilstudien,* I-II. München: Hueber, 1928.
Spitzer, Leo. *Linguistics and Literary History.* Princeton: University Press, 1948.
Spitzer, Leo. *A Method of Interpreting Literature.* Northampton, 1949.
Spurgeon, Caroline. *Shakespeare's Imagery and What It Tells Us.* Cambridge, 1935.
Steel, D. A. "Gide et Lautréamont," *RSH,* 130 (1968), 279-293.
Surréalisme en 1947 (Le). Paris: Pierre à Feu, 1947.
Tapin, Sidonia C. "Habia leido Dario a Lautréamont cuando la incluyo en *Los Raros* ?" *CL,* XI (1959), 165-170.
Ullmann, Stephen. *Style in the French Novel.* Cambridge: University Press, 1957.
Ullmann, Stephen. *The Image in the Modern French Novel.* Cambridge: University Press, 1960.
Ulmann, Stephen. "L'Image littéraire. Quelques questions de méthode," *AHC,* Paris: Les Belles Lettres, 1961.
Ullmann, Stephen. *Semantics: An Introduction to the Science of Meaning.* New York: Barnes and Noble, 1962.
Ullmann, Stephen. *Language and Style.* New York: Barnes and Noble, 1964.
Viroux, Maurice. "Lautréamont et le Dr. Chenu," *Mercure de France,* no. 1070 (Dec. 1952), 632-642.
Wann, H. V. *The Tradition of the Homeric Simile in 18th Century French Poetry.* Terre-Haute: Indiana University Press, 1931.
Weber, Jean-Paul. "Sur un thème de Maldoror," *LetN* no. 67 (1959), pp. 53-63; no. 68 (1959), pp. 238-255.
Weber, Jean-Paul. *Domaines thématiques.* Paris: Gallimard, 1963.
Wellek, René and Austin Warren. *Theory of Literature.* New York: Harcourt, Brace and Co., 1942.
Wheelwright, Philip. *Metaphor and Reality.* Bloomington: Indiana University Press, 1962.
Wimsatt, W. K., Jr. *The Verbal Icon.* New York: Noonday Press, 1960.
Zocchi, Fortunato. "L'Arte della mistificazione e la mistificazione nell'arte," *Aevum,* XXXVI (1962), 175-182.
Zweig, Paul. "Lautréamont ou les violences du Narcisse," *ALM,* 74 (1967).